Cruise
Control

By Jim Nelson

Edited by Nicholas Maier

From the files of THE NATIONAL ENQUIRER

American Media, Inc.

TOM CRUISE
Cruise Control

Copyright © 2003 AMI Books, Inc.

Cover design: Carlos Plaza
Interior design: Debbie Browning
Copy editor: Amy Persenaire

ISBN: 1-932270-25-6

First printing: December 2003

Printed in the United States of America

10 9 8 7 6 5 4 3 2 1

PROLOGUE

IT WAS STILL DARK outside that morning in 1974 when young Thomas Cruise Mapother IV felt his mother shake him awake. Mary Lee thrust a suitcase at him and told him to hurry up and get into the car. She climbed behind the wheel and hit the Canadian highway, leaving behind her husband and an unhappy life in Ottawa. Her destination was the U.S. border, then Louisville, Kentucky, then somewhere — anywhere — that was better than the life she'd known.

For Tom Mapother, just 12, his mother's flight from his father was a signature lesson, a defining moment. As he crouched in the back seat with his three sisters, watching the Ontario countryside roll by and an uncertain future grow nearer and nearer, the boy who would be Tom Cruise took note of the lessons to be learned — and learned them well.

Number one was always to know where you're going. The second was to always be the one to leave first. And the third, and most important lesson, was this: Always maintain control.

On the strength of his famous permafrost-busting smile, his sex appeal and, yes, his acting talent, Cruise has become a one-man movie conglomerate, the $25-million-per-picture man. Yet he signs every contract, every check and refuses to give lawyers a percentage of the take. Bill me by the hour, he says.

He's wrestled with directors and producers and spent hours learning their jobs — every camera angle, every piece of equipment, every production package. From the time of *Top Gun*, when he was a punk 23-year-old with one hit and a couple of so-so movies behind him, he insisted on tweaking the script, certain he knew better.

When you talk about him, you better know

what you're talking about — as those on the receiving ends of several infamous $100 million lawsuits — "weapons of terror," as one New York attorney calls them — found out quickly when they stepped on his toes and called his sexuality into question.

And when he decides something is over — let's say a marriage — it will be Tom Cruise who dictates the terms, as Nicole Kidman found out when her 10 years of wedded bliss soured and Team Tom moved in to negotiate the peace, with Tom pulling the strings in the background.

Journalists find him ingratiating — and can hardly help fawning over him — but at the same time there is little alternative, given the strong-arming of Team Tom's publicity machine, which has blazed the trail to a new era of ironclad celebrity image-shaping with Tom Cruise as its noble cause.

Cruise and his uber-publicist Pat Kingsley were early pioneers in the symbiosis between the celebrity press and Hollywood. Their game was all about control, as access to Cruise was doled out to favorite writers who, in return, agreed to keep to the script Tom and Kingsley demanded.

There was little to be left to fate, or fickle winds or whim. Even Cruise's religion, Scientology, relies less on the image of a divine being and more on its adherents using the faith's "tools" to design their own lives. Perhaps not so coincidentally, the Church of Scientology also gained notoriety for trying to assume ultimate control over what is said and printed about it, the better to control its own image.

But to a degree the control Cruise exerts has backfired. Journalists and the public sense that perhaps he sometimes protests too much. No one really believes he's gay and yet ... the false rumors won't go away.

And what really happened between Tom and Nicole that made him pull the curtain down on their supposedly happy marriage so suddenly? All Cruise has offered is the statement that Nicole "knows why" — and everybody else can get a life. He has tried to just walk on, stay in control — but still the whispers continue, dancing beyond his reach.

All of the above highlight a sense of rigidity, an inability to laugh at oneself, to throw back one's head and shake the rumors off like so much water off a duck's back. For all his control and good intentions and success, Cruise seems sometimes not so much a human but a machine, afraid of stretching, of making mistakes, of erring, of displaying real emotions.

Then again, there's no denying the essence of the Cruise appeal: the eternal boyishness, the intensity he brings to every role, the choice of roles themselves and The Smile — so bright and so full and so real that director Steven Spielberg asked Cruise not to flash it in his dour turn for *Minority Report*.

But this is not a story about a smile. It's the story of an astounding Hollywood success, of a boy who set out to have it all and who overcame a troubled, poverty-stricken childhood and succeeded beyond his wildest dreams. It's the story of an icon who has mapped his career as a star with the precision of an astronomer peering into the night sky — and who hates being brought back down to earth.

It's the story of young Thomas Cruise Mapother IV, grown up into Tom Cruise.

Chapter 1

HARDBALL

'**E**VERY LITTLE KID'S a little afraid of that hard ball when you go from T-ball to hardball," Tom Cruise has said, recalling one of his earliest, and most painful, memories. "He'd take me out there — and this guy's 6-foot-2 — and he'd just start lightly tossing the ball, then just start hammering this baseball into my glove. The ball'd be bouncing off my head. You know? Sometimes, if it hit my head, my nose would bleed and some tears would come up. He wasn't very comforting."

"This guy" was Thomas Cruise Mapother III, an electrical engineer, graduate of the University of Louisville — and bane of Tom's existence. Tom Sr. reserved a special brand of tough love for his son, born July 3, 1962, in Syracuse, New York, the third of four children Tom and Mary Lee Mapother would have.

"He was a very complex individual and created a lot of chaos in our family," Cruise said. "If I came home from a fight and I had lost, then I had to go back out there and do it again. He was one of those guys: 'You go out there and you don't lose. Period.' And I certainly wasn't the biggest guy on campus.

"He was the kind of guy who got really picked on a lot at school himself when he was growing up. He had been small, though he ended up being 6-foot-2. People had been quite brutal to him. Inside, I believe he was a really sensitive individual. He just didn't want me to have to go through the kind of pain that he had felt in his life. It ... had to do with his own way of loving me. I think that all this was a solution to solving that problem. He was very, very ... ah ... tough on me. Very, very tough. In many ways."

Cruise in the same interview said Tom Sr. abused him "physically."

"Now you'd call it abuse," Cruise said. "As a kid, I had a lot of hidden anger about that. I'd get hit and I didn't understand it. There was a lot, a lot of anger about it. Yet there was also a complexity to it, because it wasn't always like that. He could actually be quite loving."

The flip side to Tom Mapother Sr. was Tom's mom, Mary Lee. She was vivacious, positive, supportive of her children — in addition to Tom there were sisters Lee Anne, Mary and Cass — always seeing the glass half-full, no matter how hard things got. Mary Lee also had the acting bug.

"I was always interested in theater," she said once. "But I never did anything with it. When I was growing up, if you went to Hollywood, that was really risqué. I would have lost my religion, my morals, all those things that young girls thought of back then."

Mary Lee and Tom Sr. performed in local theaters wherever they moved. Cruise remembered one performance in particular.

"I remember seeing her and I remember seeing my father act in a play that they wrote together, or she wrote — an amateur thing," he said. "I was there just one day during rehearsals when they were working. I actually remember at the time thinking that my mother seemed pretty good and my father was a little stiff. But my mother, she really held herself well. She's a charismatic woman. I mean, if it wasn't for her ... I don't know why she doesn't have more gray hairs on her head. This woman is a saint."

But Tom Sr. was a macho, rough-and-tumble disciplinarian who wasn't going to raise a sissy for a son.

Years later, Cruise remembered one incident when he and his father jumped in the car to go skiing — and along the way Tom became hungry. His father refused to pull over to get his boy something to eat, instead telling his son to eat "imaginary food."

"So, we created these sandwiches," Tom Cruise said later. "It was like, 'What do you want on this sandwich?' 'What else?' 'Lettuce.' We really took a lot of time to create this sandwich and then we took a lot of time eating it. With chips and soda. And we had nothing."

From an early age, says his mother Mary Lee, Tom showed an aptitude for the theater. "He used to create skits and imitate Donald Duck and Woody Woodpecker and W.C. Fields when he was just a tiny tot."

"As a kid I used to ad-lib skits and imitations for my family," Cruise remembered. "I always enjoyed making them laugh. My mom kept saying, 'You've got so much potential. Don't give up.'"

As the only boy in a house with two older sisters, Tom remembered that there were certain benefits to the situation.

"There was a time there when my older sisters and their friends were just starting to kiss boys," he recalled. "They needed somebody to practice on. I'd sprint home from school, go in the bathroom and they'd put me on the bathroom sink and my sisters' two friends would take turns kissing me. They taught me how to French kiss when I was 8 years old. The first time I almost suffocated. I was holding my breath."

Despite those antics, Cruise does not remember his childhood fondly.

"It was very pressured, very difficult," he said. "I didn't have many friends. I mean, I had friends, but not people who really knew me. I think it made me self-destructive. I was very self-destructive when I was growing up."

Cruise blames all the moving around for much of his trouble as a kid.

"When I was a kid, we moved almost once a year," he said. "And the politics of always being the new kid in the system was very intense. The cliques, you know. You've got your Democrats over here, your Republicans over there, your country club kids, the athletes, the writers all over the place. And then there was me. I didn't fit into any group. I'd be studying American history in one school and then move to another where they're studying Cro-Magnon man. And on the day I'd show up at the new school, there would be an exam."

"If someone was new and different," he said another time, "it was just brutal. I thought, 'I can't wait to grow up because it's got to be better than this.' The politics and the fights and always wearing the wrong shoes and having the wrong accent."

Not helping matters, Tom was diagnosed at age 8 with dyslexia. His mother noticed that he had trouble reading and was copying letters from the blackboard backward.

"First, it seemed normal," he said. "I thought everyone was like this. I was also ambidextrous and in the schools I went to, it was weird or evil if you wrote with your left hand. So they made me write with my right hand, even though I naturally write with my left hand. When I speak with someone, I have a very good memory, but reading something, just getting over the words, became a big deal. My z's were backward, b's are backward, b and d, and you drop letters in writing.

"I'd try to concentrate on what I was reading, then I'd get to the end of the page and have very little memory of anything I'd read," Cruise said of his struggles in school. "I would go blank, feel anxious, nervous, bored, frustrated, dumb. I would get angry. My legs would actually hurt when I was studying. My head ached. All through school ... I felt like I had a secret. When I'd go to a new school, I wouldn't want the other kids to know about my learning disability, but then I'd be sent off to remedial reading."

Cruise remembered: "When you're a new kid, all you want to do is blend in with everything and make friends. It was a drag. It separated you and singled you out."

"My mother's dyslexic, all my sisters, too," he told another interviewer. "I had to have special reading courses. But it was something I would never tell anyone. I didn't want to be held back. But when you don't admit to something, it becomes a lot bigger than it is. I wasn't relaxed with it."

Frustrated by schoolwork, Tom poured his energies into sports. "I would pick up a new sport as a way to make friends," he said. "I'd go up and say, 'Do you play tennis? Do you want to play sometime?'"

Tom Sr.'s job finally landed the family in Ottawa, Canada — where ice hockey is the national pastime. Young Tom naturally wanted to join the other boys out on the rinks — and he had to override his mother's objections.

"I remember when I moved to Canada and I had figure skates and I wanted to play ice hockey," he said. "And my mother said, 'Listen, you're going to get your teeth knocked out' and just did not want me playing hockey. I ended up proving to her that I could. I would be out there

at night, right after school, early in the morning, just teaching myself how to skate."

"That was a sport I was really concerned about
because of the violence," Mary Lee remembered.
"Then one of his teeth got knocked out — at tennis
practice! With the instructor standing right
there!"

Hockey. Tennis. Lacrosse. Football. Soccer.
Cruise excelled at every sport he tried, as if his
body was making up for the troubles his mind
had in school.

But sports couldn't solve everything. Tom's
parents weren't getting along. And at the age of
12, he was to become, for all intents and
purposes, the man of the Mapother family.

Chapter 2

RUN

TOM AND MARY LEE MAPOTHER sat their four children down one day in 1974 and dropped the bombshell: They were getting divorced. Everyone cried — even hard-as-nails Tom Mapother Sr.

Cruise would remember that hearing the news from his parents was like hearing that a loved one had died. Children can tell when their parents aren't getting along — but

hearing the word "divorce" had the finality of
death.

Tom Sr. took his son outside to hit some base-
balls afterward, but Tom was crying too hard to
see the ball. Despite the troubles he'd had with
his dad, the thought of him not being there was
hard to grasp. He says he kept thinking, "What's
going to happen to us now? What next?"

Mary Lee Mapother, though, was in a hurry to
get herself and her children away from her
husband. She wanted to get her kids out of the
country without Tom Sr. finding out. "I think with
Canadian law," Tom said later, "he could've kept us
in the country if he found out we were leaving."

For a week, she told her children to keep their
things packed. Tom packed his baseball glove and
a few clothes — and one morning at 4:30 a.m.,
after Tom Sr. had already left for work, Mary Lee
and the kids made a dash for the border. Mary Lee
alternately cried, sang and laughed her way south
that day. She would later remember the divorce as
"a time of growing, a time of conflict."

Tom remembered that time more grimly. "We
felt like fugitives," he said. He would see his father
only two more times before Tom Sr.'s death in 1984.

Resettling in Kentucky, Tom quickly assumed
the duties of the man of the family. But the divorce
cast a pall across his youth and the family's continued pattern of moving to find work didn't help.

"My parents' divorce had a huge impact on me when I was 12," he said. "I went through a period, after the divorce, of really wanting to be accepted, wanting love and attention from people. But I never really seemed to fit in anywhere.

"And traveling the way I did, you're closed off a lot from people. I didn't express a lot to people where I moved. They didn't have the childhood I had and I didn't feel like they'd understand me.

"I think it made me self-destructive. I was very self-destructive when I was growing up. I was always looking for attention. I'd get into fights, get suspended from school. I think it was out of a need to be creative. Because if you can't create, you eventually start to destroy yourself."

Looking back, Cruise said all the moving around, the difficulty in fitting in, may have been responsible for his eventual movie career.

"In every different place, I became a different person," he said. "You've got to create your own world when you move like that. That was just my way of dealing with things."

If there was a silver lining in all the doom and gloom, it was that Mary Lee had a close, warm nuclear family unit, finally free of Tom Sr.

"Even the troubled moments were quite exciting," Cruise remembered. "I look back on it and our family was very close. The rough times really brought us together. My mother had to raise four kids. We kept moving around. I think I went to something like 15 schools. There was no money, but I know people who had it 100 times worse than we did. You just have to go out there and survive. I just looked at it as an adventure."

"He's always been more of my big brother, rather than my little brother," his sister Lee Anne said. "He was very caring and protective of us. Whenever any of us girls started dating anybody we were serious about, having them meet Tom was a big deal. His opinion always weighed very heavily with all of us."

"My sister Mary couldn't figure out for years why this guy wouldn't kiss her," Tom remembered. "Well, because I told him not to. The guy was a year older than me, but I said, 'If you kiss my sister, I'm going to kill you, man.' Because I knew he had another girlfriend. But poor Mary, she just wanted this guy to kiss her and couldn't figure it out."

Mary Lee worked any kind of job she could find to support her children. "You know, women have dreams of having careers and being whatever," Mary Lee said later. "I had a dream of raising children and enjoying them and having a good family life."

Tom got a paper route and the girls pitched in as well. "With my mother working, my sisters all cooked," he said. "Since they were 7 years old, they cooked for the whole family. We were a team and we went through a lot together, going to different schools. There were lots of fights, too — women in the morning."

Tom continued to struggle with school — and excel at sports. Even though he was now far south of the Canadian border, he picked up where he left off and played hockey.

"He was so fast they couldn't keep up with him," Mary Lee said. "One guy finally got so exasperated that he picked Tom up by the scruff of the neck and the seat of his pants and moved him outside the boundary. I laughed!"

Tom tried to help his mother, who was scrambling to make ends meet with no support coming from Tom Sr. — who, for reasons never fully explained, had been cut off from communication with his family.

Things were tight. The family remembers one Christmas when there was no money to buy gifts, so Mary Lee and her children wrote poems to one another and read them out loud.

Another time, Mary Lee was forced to apply for food stamps. "She saw all these people and she said, 'I don't care what it takes, I'm not going to come here again,' " Cruise recalled. "So she just did everything she could to feed us. And we made it. We made it. My father didn't pay child support. Once my mother divorced my father, it was just four women and myself."

But there was unconditional love — finally. Tom credits his mother for helping him find a way to get through high school despite his dyslexia.

"She worked three jobs and took care of my sisters and me, but with everything she had on her plate, she would also work with me," Tom said. "If I had to write an assignment for school, I would dictate it to her first, then she would write it down and I would copy it very carefully."

Tom also devised his own methods to get by in class, although he could barely read the blackboard.

"I went to three different high schools, so I was always given the benefit of the doubt for being the new kid," he said. "And I had different techniques for getting by in class. I raised my hand a lot. I knew that if I participated, I'd get extra points and could pass. If I had a test in the afternoon, I'd find kids at lunchtime who'd taken the test that morning and find out what it was like.

"I was a functional illiterate. I loved learning, I wanted to learn, but I knew I had failed in the system. Like a lot of people, though, I had figured out how to get through it."

But Tom has no fond memories of his schooling. "I remember walking to school one time with my sisters and saying, 'Let's just get through this. If we can just get through this somehow' ... I look back on high school and grade school and I would never want to go back there. Not in a million years."

At age 14, Tom entered a Franciscan seminary on a scholarship.

"More than anything, it had to do with the fact that our family didn't have enough money to feed me," he said. "When you're a kid, you really feel the pressure to lighten it up. We didn't have any money for school and it was a good, free education. They even clothed you.

"It was such a tough time. I needed a focus in my life, something that was consistent. I was looking for structure."

But being away from his family was tough — for everyone. "It was tough, but it was good, because it was my first time really away from home," he said. "My sisters used to drive up to see me and they would cry all the way home because they missed me."

Cruise said the year in the monastery was his best, school-wise. "I really got a solid education that year," he said. "It was actually the best year I did in school."

But Cruise was not cut out to be a priest and returned to public school after his freshman year. "I realized I didn't want to be a priest," he said. "I realized I loved women too much to give that up. Even at that age, I was too interested in ladies."

"We used to sneak out of school on weekends and go to this girl's house, sit around, talk and play spin the bottle," he said.

Considering he had three sisters with lots of girlfriends tracking through the house, he was pretty well versed in the ways of women. "Three sisters ... sisters have friends ... things happen," he laughed. "Wonderful, magical things happen. You started out with your older sisters' friends and then as the years went on it was the younger sister's friends."

One girlfriend, however, remembered Tom as being shy — which forced her to make the first move.

"He was just one of the gang who always seemed to be hanging around, but he was cute," said Laurie Hobbs in 1990. "He was so shy. He was always so self-conscious about his teeth. In fact, he used to have a chipped front tooth that embarrassed him so much he had it fixed."

Laurie remembered that she was the one who had to ask Tom, then a sophomore in high school, to a school dance. That night, they wound up at a friend's house.

"I got things going by casually dropping my hand on the couch beside him, so it was easy to find," she said. "Then I just inched it along until it touched his hand. I can hardly describe how excited I was when he took hold of my hand at last. We sort of lunged at each other awkwardly and started kissing. My head was spinning and I could hardly breathe. Once or twice I opened my eyes to make sure his eyes were closed and they were, so I was sure he meant it."

Shortly afterward, Tom Sr. tracked the family down, showing up one day at their door in Louisville. He invited Tom and one of his sisters to a drive-in movie. But the trip, it turned out, was designed as an attempt to sweet-talk Mary Lee into coming back to him. She declined.

By the time Tom Sr. made his move to reclaim his wife and family, Mary Lee had met a man named Jack South at an electronics convention. When Tom was 16, Mary Lee remarried and the family settled — once and for all — in Glen Ridge, New Jersey.

Tom remembered having his own Oedipus complex as his mother found love. "In the beginning, I felt threatened by my stepfather," he said. "There's a part of you that's in love with your mother. But he is such a wise, smart man. He loved my mother so much that he took us all in, four young people. We'd bet on football games and he was a terrible bettor, so I'd make lots of money."

By now, Tom was in his senior year of high school — and it looked like he would get through it after all. He credits his tough childhood for developing his now-legendary need for control, his need to survive above all.

"When you have to cope with a lot of problems, you are either going to sink or you are going to swim," he said. "You're either going to take the challenge and rise to the occasion or it's just going to devour you. You just make that choice. Am I going to survive? Or am I going to be eaten alive? And I was trying to survive the best I could."

Tom continued with sports and had taken up wrestling to go with baseball, hockey and football. He had no idea what he would do once he got out of high school, but he knew he had a love for the movies — especially *Midway* and *Star Wars*.

While cutting a neighbor's lawn, Tom rushed through to make it to *Midway*. "This woman kind of complained I wasn't doing a good job on her yard," he said. "And I said, 'Look, I'll finish it later. You don't understand. *Midway*! The airplanes!' "

He hadn't connected the dots — yet. "If I could just focus in and do something," he remembered thinking, "I know I've got the energy and creativity to be great."

When a knee injury prevented him from wrestling his senior year, Tom's glee club instructor told him he should try out for the school production of *Guys and Dolls*. Tom wound up getting the lead part of Nathan Detroit.

"I can't describe the feeling that was there," Tom's frustrated thespian mother Mary Lee remembered about opening night. "It was just an incredible experience to see what we felt was a lot of talent coming forth all of a sudden. It had been dormant for so many years — not thought of or talked about or discussed in any way."

Tom felt the same feeling coursing through him that night. A light went off in his head: "All of a sudden you are up there and you're doing something you really enjoy and you are getting all this attention and people who never turned their heads or said anything before are now saying, 'Gee. Look at him.' And I said to myself, 'This is it.' As soon as I started acting, I felt, from that point on, that if I didn't go for this, I would be making a terrible mistake."

"After the show, Tom came home and said he wanted to have a talk with my husband and me," Mary Lee recalled. "He asked for 10 years to give show business a try. Meanwhile, my husband's thinking, 'What's this gonna cost me? Ten years of what?' "

Now, she adds, "It's a kind of a joke in the family. Sort of a joke and not a joke. At any rate,

Tom said, 'Let me see. I really feel that this is what I want to do.' And we both wholeheartedly agreed, because we both felt it was a God-given talent and he should explore it because he was so enthused about it. So to make a long story short, we gave him our blessing — and the rest is history."

Chapter 3

THE POSER

I MAGINE IF YOU'D INVESTED in Tom Cruise stock in 1980. His stepfather bought in on the ground floor with an $850 loan to the wannabe actor — but settled for a repayment of the principal.

Tom skipped his high school graduation ceremony to appear in a local production of *Godspell*. And with summer in full bloom, he headed for New York. There had been little discussion about going to college. After struggling mightily just to stay afloat throughout grade school and then high school, formal schooling took backstage.

"We had to pay for our own educations," he said. "If you stayed at home, you had to pay room and board. You had to contribute. I'd been to so many different schools. I wasn't hungry for more schooling, formal education, at that point. I didn't have a lot of money anyway; it would have been a waste of money. I always thought I'd go back, though."

A classmate hooked him up with a manager in New York, and he and Mary Lee headed up the New Jersey Turnpike to destiny.

That first manager was Tobe Gibson, owner of the Young Talent agency. "He was very young, 16 1/2, when he signed with me," she said. "He told me he had done *Guys and Dolls* in high school and that was it. But even though he was untested, I saw something in Tom."

Gibson took credit for Tom's name change as well. "He had just come to New York from Louisville and was living in New Jersey," she recalled. "He had no money. But I manage lots of young talent. So I changed his name from Tom Mapother to Tom Cruise and took him on."

"So now I have this manager in New York, and I took my mom ... and we drove to New York,"

Cruise said. "I remember we drove in this old green Pinto I paid 50 bucks for. It was rush hour and my mother and I had an argument about something. I think the two of us weren't talking, and because I was 17, I couldn't get a manager unless my mother co-signed for me. So she gets in the car and we're going to New York, and I don't have any pictures or anything, and I just ran up to this manager's office. I told my mother, 'Just park the car somewhere.' And I went up to meet this woman.' "

Tom got a quick lesson in what life was going to be like on acting's bottom rung.

"She had me read for this Hershey commercial," he recalled. "And, you know, it was one of those, 'Yeah, yeah, yeah, babe, you're beautiful, I'm going to make you a star' sort of situations. And I started out with this person.

"I remember she would call me into New York — this was even before I graduated — and say we were going to have a very important meeting. And I'd get to the city and she'd ask me to run errands or go grocery shopping for her. So after a month of that, I wanted to fire her. And she said, 'Well, you can't.' I had signed a five-year contract. Thank God, I was only 17. I just called a lawyer and got another manager."

After moving permanently to New York that summer, Tom did get some schooling — he caught acting workshops at the Neighborhood Playhouse when he could. "It was great," he recalled of his time in the Big Apple. "I was like an animal in the jungle. I didn't have enough money to buy food, so I'd walk to my classes — save that $1.25 so I could buy hot dogs and rice."

For a year and a half, he bused tables, unloaded trucks and even became the assistant superintendent of his apartment building.

"People would call me in the middle of the night and say, 'My heating's not working,' " he recalled. "And I'd say, 'Well, my f***ing heating's not working, either.' "

"I've always supported myself," he said. "I'm a survivor. So I thought I'd work any way I could: busing tables, unloading trucks. It always seemed that whenever I was down to my last penny, something came up."

Cruise said he wasn't necessarily thinking of becoming a movie star. "I never really thought of movies," he said. "I just wanted to be an artist, an actor. I read for plays. I just enjoyed working on characters."

Like all young actors in New York, he went to readings. And more readings. But early on, he found producers pushing him toward film.

"I was reading for this television thing," he said, "and this executive said to me, 'You know, you're just too intense and you're not pretty enough for television. You ought to think about features.' I guess I'm kind of an obsessive person when I'm working on something. I used to go up for TV commercials and I never got those things, either. They always said I was too intense: 'Eat the Fritos!' "

He soon found the cold underbelly of showbiz. "I was up for a situation comedy, and some network brought me out to California," he said. "I had just finished reading and the guy said to me, 'How long are you gonna be out here?' And I was thinking, 'I kicked ass in this reading — this guy's gonna call me for a callback.' And I said, 'Oh, about a week or so.' 'Oh, a week,' he said. 'Well, get a tan while you're here.' It was just so cold. I walked out and I thought to myself, 'Did that really happen?' "

It's the old cliché: The struggling young actor or actress in New York, busing tables, eating peanut butter sandwiches, rushing from cattle call to cattle call. But Cruise stood out above the rest, whether it was the smile that would become so famous or just sheer ability. He had something — and within five months of hitting the New York bricks, he had his first film role, a Brooke Shields vehicle called *Endless Love* (1981).

Tom played Billy, whose friend David has been forbidden from seeing Jade (Shields). On the advice of Billy, David sets fire to Jade's home in a misguided attempt to heroically save the family and win the right to be with Jade. Besides Cruise, other newcomers in the film were James Spader (Jimmy Spader in the credits) and Jami Gertz.

Tom's first line? "Hey, I tried that — I ever tell you guys? Eight years old and I was into arson." He said it while taking off his T-shirt, exposing the rippling 18-year-old abs he developed playing high school sports. It was a small scene, but it was a beginning.

"I didn't even know what a camera was I was so green," he recalled.

Also beginning at this point, it seems, were the false gay rumors that plague him to this day. Tom unwittingly agreed to pose — fully clothed — for pictures that would ultimately turn up in a gay magazine called *Parlee*. Tom appeared shirtless in one photo with his legs open toward the camera. In another, he had his hands on his waist and wore crotch-hugging mini-shorts.

Even though Tom is not gay, one publishing insider said, "I think these photos were carefully posed by the photographer to appeal to a gay audience. And because Tom is so young — without evidence of body or facial hair — they also would appeal to the 'chicken hawk,' an older gay man interested in young boys."

The magazine that the photos ended up in, *Parlee*, was a strictly gay magazine distributed only in men's bars and clubs in the New York

City area. "The fact that Tom posed for the photos may be the origin of questions that have wrongly persisted over his sexual preference. It would certainly help explain why the false rumors started."

Tom was still in the live-and-learn mode — and wouldn't understand the repercussions of his innocent modeling for years. But his next film would raise him head and shoulders above the thousands of wannabes pounding the pavement in New York and Los Angeles and allow him to skip any more day rates for model shoots.

Director Harold Becker chose Tom to play a small role as a military cadet in 1981's *Taps*, which already had Timothy Hutton and Sean Penn headlining. Cruise was so ecstatic to have more than one day's work that he splurged on himself.

"They were giving me three meals a day and a cash per diem," he said. "You could go out and buy your own food. I'd worked as a kid for, like, $2, $2.50 an hour — but they were handing me $100 in cash! I remember there was a place up the street that served steak and lobster. I'd only had lobster once in my life before that. I'd go there every night and I'd call my family: 'I'm eating steak and lobster every night!' "

Cruise's equal enthusiasm for the small role he'd been cast in — as a sidekick to hothead cadet

David Shawn — forced the director to reconsider him for a larger role that had already gone to another actor.

"Cruise was so strong that the other guy didn't have a chance," Sean Penn said. "Very intense, 200 percent there. It was overpowering — and we'd all kind of laugh, because it was so sincere. Good acting, but so far in the intense direction that it was funny."

Cruise at first didn't want to take on the part of David Shawn, the ill-tempered and aggressive co-leader of the cadets, who attempt to save their academy from being bulldozed. When approached by Becker, Cruise says, "I just thought, 'Oh, f**k.' I said, 'Thank you very much, but I don't think I want to play David Shawn.' I was in a small role and that's the way I wanted it to be. I was learning so much just by being around, watching everything that was happening."

"Tom told the producer, 'If this isn't all right with the other actors, I don't want to do it,'" Penn said. "To the end he was like that. He really was a total innocent."

"He just wasn't doing his job," Cruise acknowledged of the unnamed actor whose failure paved the way for Tom's success. "He wasn't taking it seriously. I remember saying, 'Get it together, man! What are you doing here?' And when it didn't work out, I felt bad for him."

Sean Penn remembered the producers giving Cruise a take-it-or-take-a-hike ultimatum. "The producers just told him, 'Look, buddy, if you don't want to do it, leave. We want you for this part, but we're not gonna beg you.' So the next day he took it. It was incredible how innocent and naïve he was when he came in to do *Taps*."

Cruise was a basket case, worrying that his whole future was riding on the character of David Shawn.

"I remember during *Taps*, I couldn't sleep at night sometimes. I thought, 'OK, I want to be an actor. I want to learn about what acting is.' I had this feeling of, 'Here I am 18 years old and this stuff is going on.' I thought, 'Do I have what it takes?' That's a very scary proposition, because I felt I don't know what I'm going to do. I'm going to give it everything I have, because I love this and I want to be able to get good at this."

He threw himself into the role — even going the extra mile to pump up physically, adding 15 pounds to his wiry frame by swigging milk-shakes. Bigger, David Shawn became even more menacing.

Cruise got good reviews working next to the already established Penn and Hutton. And even more significant, he managed to scrape together enough money to pay his stepfather back — with interest.

"Saved my money, brought him down, paid him off with interest," Cruise recalled. "Good man. That was great, paying him back all the money."

Just 18 and still innocent, Tom Cruise was finding his path — but that's not to say there weren't detours.

Cruise now calls his next film, *Losin' It,* "my cable classic." But in 1982, it was work.

"You know you're in trouble when it's a comedy and everybody making the movie is miserable," he said. Co-starring Shelley Long in her pre-*Cheers* days, the film was a "first-time-in-Tijuana titillator," according to one alliterative writer.

But Cruise said he wanted to play against the type he had established in *Taps.*

"I didn't know anything about this business," he said. "I thought everybody wanted to make great movies. I'd just come off a terrific experience — you know, working with Hutton, who'd just won the Academy Award — and I get this call saying, 'You've just been offered this movie and it's gonna be the next big movie.' I didn't like the script, but I hadn't read that many. I wasn't real educated in them. So I ventured into it with total commitment and it, uh, was a nightmare. But I learned a lot from it. I realized that if you wanna grow as an actor, you have to work with the best people. Then you'll be able to have more control over what you do."

"That's an important film for me," Cruise added, looking back. "I can look at it and say, 'Thank God, I've grown.' I thought anyone could make a great movie — all you had to do was knock yourself out. I didn't know anything about anything."

Chapter 4

ALL BUSINESS

B Y THE TIME *TAPS* CAME out in theaters, Cruise was living in West Hollywood. He had made friends with Tim Hutton and Sean Penn, and became part of the social world revolving around Sean and his brother Chris Penn.

"Those were some wild times," Cruise remembered. But he was looking for more than just prowling the town as an eligible and newly wealthy bachelor. "My life just wasn't full," he said. "It was very difficult to try to find where to go and what to do. Very unsettled."

However, he added, "One thing I did know: I had enough discipline and conviction in what I was doing to be an actor."

Tom found an ally in his attempt to get settled, to stay the course of his career. Her name was Paula Wagner, a Hollywood agent. Tom signed on with her — and remains with her to this day. Tom explained his career goals to her at their first meeting: He wanted to work with the top people, always be looking to grow his career and not have to worry about the money.

Wagner teamed Cruise with legendary director Francis Ford Coppola — auteur of *The Godfather* films — in *The Outsiders*.

The film was shot in Tulsa, Oklahoma, and co-starred some of the best young talent in Hollywood at the time: Diane Lane, Emilio Estevez, Rob Lowe and Matt Dillon, in a tale of gang warfare between the preppy Socials and the Greasers. Cruise, playing a Greaser, had a cap removed from his front tooth — the one broken by the tennis ball — and went without showering for most of the nine-week shoot to keep that, well, greasy feeling.

Tom showed his prowess for pranks while the cast and crew stayed at the Tulsa Excelsior Hotel.

Tom wrote "Helter Skelter" on Diane Lane's hotel mirror and smeared honey on her toilet seat. In return, he found a bag of dog doo-doo on the doorknob of his room, courtesy of Estevez. But for a group of young actors playing a group of wild, young roustabouts in the film, "it worked for the character," Cruise laughed.

"There was this bellman in Chicago I ran into recently and he said, 'Mr. Cruise, I was in the Excelsior when you were there.' And I said, 'Oh, my God!'"

By this time, Cruise was working steadily, getting noticed, hanging out with elements of the Brat Pack. Still, he was no star. But that was about to change.

Wagner brought him the role of Joel Goodson, a suburban boy who uses his parents' upscale digs to run a prostitution business while they're away in Paul Brickman's *Risky Business*. It was considered a small film, and there were small expectations for it, but it was a starring role for Cruise. He made the most of the opportunity, becoming a cultural icon on the film's release in 1983 when audiences caught him dancing — in his underwear, no less — through the house to the beat of Bob Seger's *Old Time Rock & Roll*.

"I taught myself how to dance after *Saturday Night Fever* — you know, the big thing was to go

to these dance places on Sunday nights and we
would go and dance with the girls," Cruise said.
"The only way to meet the girls was if you were a
really good dancer. So I learned by watching
American Bandstand and *Soul Train* and stuff.
It obviously worked." He explained the scene's
appeal this way: "With kids, to be a rock star is
the ultimate. When their parents leave, they
turn the music up. Dancing with your pants off
— it's total freedom."

The scene was just one line in the script — "Joel
dances in underwear through the house." Cruise
made a career out of the scene — and it became
part of the culture, as evidenced when Ron
Reagan Jr., parodied it on *Saturday Night Live*.

"Paul showed me the opening frame and said,
'I want you to use the whole living room,' "
Cruise said. "We talked about it. It was my idea
to use the candlestick as a microphone. First I
tried jumping into the frame, then I waxed the
floor and threw some dirt around so I could slide
perfectly into the center of the opening shot,
give it that first beat. Really, the whole thing was
just Paul and I playing."

Ironically, Cruise was not the first choice for the
role. Director Brickman, he said, "didn't want to
see me for *Risky Business* — at least this is what I
heard — because he'd seen *Taps*," Cruise said.

Cruise left Oklahoma midway through *The*

Outsiders to meet with Brickman in Los Angeles. Cruise remembered being "pumped up and talking in an Oklahoma accent. Paul just sat there."

The two got around to a reading at the meeting and after a slow start ended up doing half the movie. "It was fun, we were all laughing," Cruise said. Though Cruise and the already-cast female lead, Rebecca De Mornay, did not "test" well, Cruise got the part, and became fast friends with Brickman, to boot.

Cruise and his co-star, Rebecca De Mornay, did not hit it off. Though still something of an unknown, Cruise had the temerity to try to have De Mornay, who was cast over Michelle Pfeiffer, axed from the film. He complained to Brickman and the film's producers that things weren't "working" between him and De Mornay.

"We explained to Tom that, from our point of view, she was not going to be replaced and that she was doing a terrific job," producer Steve Tisch later said. "We told him that as production went on, they were going to have to play a number of scenes together and there had to be this illusion these two characters were falling in love."

It was the first instance of Cruise trying to exert the control he would become famous for — and he lost. But he and Brickman squabbled about little else.

"It seemed like he and Paul were kind of a

unit," co-star De Mornay said of Cruise and Brickman. "They would show up on the set in the morning wearing exactly the same clothes: the jeans, the sweaters, the loafers. It was Tom's outfit for the movie, but it just happened to coincide with Paul's real-life wardrobe. They were both Joel, as far as I could see."

Tom ran off 14 pounds in the Florida sun for the role, then stopped exercising to add a layer of baby fat. "He's a very vulnerable person," Cruise said. "I didn't want any physical defenses up for him. No muscle armor at all."

De Mornay played a hooker, and she and Tom became involved in reel life — and in real life. Two days after trying to get De Mornay booted, he told producer Steve Tisch he didn't need his hotel room any longer — because he and De Mornay had moved in together!

But their passion didn't translate to the screen as easily as all involved had hoped. A love scene had to be re-shot and Brickman decided to place it in one of Chicago's elevated trains.

"We had another love scene, but it just didn't work," Cruise said. "It just didn't ... wasn't really, uh, erotic." The 'el' scene, shot after the rest of the picture had wrapped, was a success — but Cruise found it tough going.

"I remember it was just uncomfortable," he said. "A love scene can step over the line sometimes. I don't mean that I step over the line or that the other person steps over the line — it's just, how far do you go? And although it may be exciting and romantic for the audience — you hope it is, otherwise you're doing it for nothing — it's just kind of uncomfortable."

Tom may have been uncomfortable doing it, but the scene sizzled onscreen. One writer said of the scene: "Masterfully shot and edited to the music of Tangerine Dream, the scene gave *Risky Business* a genuine touch of lyrical eroticism."

Shortly after the scene was shot, Tom and Rebecca went public with their romance. For Tom, De Mornay was his first, real longtime relationship. "During the film, we did have a strong affinity for each other," De Mornay said. "But it was, like, not the same."

Some of that affinity came from their backgrounds. Like Cruise, Rebecca had moved around a lot. "We have very similar backgrounds," she said at the time, "with all the moving around and stuff, except that mine was through Europe and his was through the United States."

But more than that, De Mornay noted that Tom seemed to be looking for someone to love — and to love him back. "He really is a pure person," she said. "There's something earnest and virtuous about him that's quite rare. There's definitely something different about kids who come from broken homes. They have this sort of searching quality, because you're searching for love and affection, if you've been robbed of a substantial amount of time with your parents. I think that's true with Tom."

Risky Business earned a whopping $65 million and was a certified hit with the new MTV generation. Everyone except Cruise seemed to be surprised by the film's success. "I wasn't," he said. "You just feel it when you're making a good movie. The script was so well-written and Brickman had such integrity. It could have gone totally the other way. The film really rides that line."

The critics liked it, one saying Cruise occupied the film "the way Dustin Hoffman occupied *The Graduate*." The gossip columns started noticing him and his romance with De Mornay only turned up the heat, as paparazzi staked out their New York City hotel hoping for shots. "The public," one writer noted, "started discovering how wholesome, gracious and kind he could be."

Tom Cruise, movie star, was making all the right moves — including his next film, *All the Right Moves*. Though the film — about a Pennsylvania high school football player's struggle with his coach and his future — wasn't a big production, it was another step in the right direction for the young Cruise.

The intense star showed up early to the

Johnstown, Pennsylvania, location. He dyed his
hair, attended high school under an assumed
name to get a feel for his high school character
and worked out with the football team.

Further keeping in tune with his character,
Cruise stepped up as a leader on the production
and proved he was willing to assert himself with
the producers. He organized acting workshops
off the set and to co-star Lea Thompson's delight,
he fought with the producers and got them to
limit the amount of nudity required of her for her
role as girlfriend to his character Stef Djordevic.

All The Right Moves was a serious drama, like
Taps. And Cruise, the actor, was taken very seriously by reviewers. Cruise "makes Stef honest
and believable, though in Stef's hotter-tem-
pered scenes Mr. Cruise seems overly mild," said
The New York Times. "He's better at presenting
Stef's worried, tentative side than at conveying
the discipline and determination through
which Stef hopes to succeed."

Another reviewer noted that the performance
as Stef proved that Cruise was "the most sophis-
ticated, the most appealing, the most capable of
tackling a wider dramatic range." Cruise, Rex
Reed wrote, was "an actor, not a talking poster."

Hardly 21 years old, Tom Cruise made the
climb to the top look so easy. He was getting good
reviews and good box office — *Moves* earned $17

million. The role solidified Cruise's standing at the top of Hollywood's young actors. He could demand $1 million a film and huge things were expected of him.

Then he disappeared.

Chapter 5

LEGENDS

TOM WAS IN LOS ANGELES in 1984 preparing to go to London for his next project when the phone rang. "You know how sometimes the phone rings and — ping! — you just know," he said.

The news hit Cruise hard — his father, Thomas Cruise Mapother III, was dead.

Though they'd been estranged for years, it's exactly those kinds of circumstances that can make a death all the worse. There's no more time for reconciliation. Cruise, though, did have the solace of having reached out to his dad. In late 1983, *Risky Business* was a hit and *All the Right Moves* had just come out, Cruise and his siblings put aside their hard feelings and visited their father in the hospital as he recovered from a cancer operation.

"All four of my children showed up at the hospital and all I could do was cry," Thomas Sr. said. "That's how bad the strain has been because of the divorce situation. It had been about four or five years — a long time, at least to me."

Tom Sr. had seen pictures of his only son in the newspapers, but could hardly believe that was Tom Jr. "I couldn't believe it when he walked in the room," Tom Sr. said. "I was a little concerned that I wouldn't see my son, because I'd seen a lot of the pictures in the paper and the publicity shots. And that wasn't my son. He walked into the room ... and I knew who he was. What those kids did for me, I could never explain."

"He allowed me to go to the hospital to talk to him under the condition of not asking him any questions," Cruise said of that meeting. "But he said to me before he died, 'Look, I'm gonna get better and you and me are gonna go and have a steak and a beer and talk about the whole thing.'" Unfortunately, that dinner never happened.

"I loved my father very much," Cruise said years after his Dad had passed away. "My father never saw any of my movies before he died, but he had pictures of me on the wall in his hospital room. He told the nurses how he had made a mistake with me and my sisters."

But Tom Sr.'s death "cleared up a lot of kind of fog that I had about the man," Cruise said. "I think that he felt remorse for a lot that had happened. He was a person who did not have a huge influence on me in my teens; the values and motivation really came from my stepfather. But he was important. Really important. It's all sort of complex. There wasn't one thing I felt."

After the funeral, Tom left for London to shoot *Legend*, a fanciful Ridley Scott film full of unicorns and hobbit-type imagery and characters, including Tom's — Jack O'Lantern, an old-style hero who must defeat darkness itself and allow the sun to prevail on Earth.

"After what I was going through emotionally, facing death and all of that, somehow it was important for me to try to get back to the innocence within my own soul," he said. "I'm just glad I had acting then. I don't know what I would have done without my work. It gave me a place to deal with all those emotions."

Cruise had been happy to sign on — "I'm a huge fan of Ridley Scott," he said — but had his doubts about the picture before he left the States. "Two months before we started filming, I called my agent about it," he said. "She asked if I wanted her to get me out of the film. And I said no. I remember my father had just died and I was like ... I had this thing, like I had to go through it."

Filming was a disaster. The set burned down. Cruise, his hair grown down to his shoulders for the role, spent long hours in his trailer doing nothing. But he says he learned some valuable lessons.

"It was such a test of my endurance and patience," Cruise said. "It would take a week to shoot a scene that in the film would be 30 seconds. Then sometimes I would sit in my dressing room for a week and a half — be called in every morning and not leave till late — and just sit there."

The fire caused months of delays. Tom walked around London, hung out — learned to deal with the situation. "I really had to make a choice," he recalled. "When the set burned down, it was like, 'What are we going to do now? Where does this take us?' I said, 'I can sit here and feel sh**ty and wallow in my frustration, or I can just come in every day.' Instead of getting frustrated and banging your head against the wall, you say, 'OK, that happened, now what do we do? Let's go ahead.' "

He added: "I mean, I always had that ability to deal with things. My whole life has been like that: 'OK, what do I do now?' "

And in the end, Cruise would value his time on *Legend*, although it was a dud and ran in a truncated, 89-minute version in the United States. He wasn't surprised.

"You know when you're playing it, the character isn't there," Cruise said. "But as you go along you learn a lot — you learn what scripts not to do. It's the bottom line: If it ain't on the page, it ain't on the stage."

The film earned $15 million and fared no better with critics than it did with moviegoers. "*Legend* does not work," wrote one reviewer. "To some degree, this is a fairy tale, and it needs a certain lightness of tone, a plucky cheerfulness, to work." As for Cruise, "I particularly noticed how easily Cruise got buried in the role of Jack," the reviewer wrote. "Here is the talented young actor from *Risky Business*, where he came across as a genuine individual, and this time he's so overwhelmed by sets and special effects that his character could be played by anybody."

Cruise actually agreed. "I don't think Ridley Scott necessarily needed me to do the movie," he said. "It could have been anyone in that part. Coming out of *Legend*, I was extremely hungry to work with a group of actors, to start really breaking down scenes again and getting involved on that level, real characters."

He was also eager to spend more time with

De Mornay — but found his separation from her while making the film had caused the relationship to die. They broke up when Cruise returned to the States.

"Like everything, people get to the point where you go your different ways," he said. "I was just going in a different direction. It wasn't like, 'Hey, shake hands. It's been great, baby. Let's have lunch.' When you care about someone that deeply, it's always difficult, but it wasn't ugly or anything."

Though obviously upset by the breakup, Cruise at the time was philosophical. He was getting wise beyond his years.

"Relationships are hard," he said in 1986. "You have to know when you're going to be in a different place from someone else, you have to have the strength to separate. People are more prone to stay together for the security, which is something in my life that I have really not done, in relationships or even in business. If something's not working, you've got to face it and move on."

Tom would show an awesome ability to do just that — move on — in the years to come. But, in 1985, the concern was his career more than his love life. He had achieved one goal: He was working steadily as an actor. And the disaster of *Legend* and his absence from the United States did not, at least, harm his career for long. Before anyone hardly noticed he was gone, Cruise came roaring back.

Chapter 6

FLYING

BEVERLY HILLS COP PRODUCERS Don Simpson and Jerry Bruckheimer got the idea for what would become *Top Gun* from an article about the elite flying school at Miramar Naval Air Station down the coast in San Diego. The article in *California* magazine focused on the Navy pilots and Bruckheimer said he and Simpson instantly caught that the fliers were "rock and rollers in the sky. They looked like American Stings: these guys with these shocks of blond and black hair, with nicknames like Yogi and Possum and Radar. And it was all real."

They commissioned a script and got the cooperation of the Navy to use its facilities and know-how to film the movie. The producers' first choice for the role of the hero was Matthew Modine, but he passed. A script was sent to Cruise, still in London doing *Legend*. He was interested — but not overly enthused.

"I liked it," Cruise recalled. "But it needed a lot of work."

Once back in the States, Cruise met with the producers and felt better about the project. "I felt like they had that fighter-pilot spirit," he said. "The top gun, the best of the best."

Cruise, 23 years old and fresh off a disaster, made a grab for more control of the project. Not wanting to go through another experience like *Legend* — ever — Cruise said he didn't want to commit to the project until after he'd worked on the script.

"*Top Gun* had an idea for a character and, yes, the first script wasn't good," he said. "But you just look for an idea for the character and that's what you start with. You get involved and you make it work.

"I said, 'After two months, if I don't want to do

it, the script's gonna be in good enough shape,
and you'll have more of a sense of what you
want to do ... There are other actors,' " Cruise
said. "I think they were kind of taken aback at
first. But after coming off of *Legend*, I just
wanted to make sure everything was gonna go
the way we talked about it."

Years later, Cruise laughed about his audacity,
but Bruckheimer and Simpson agreed to let
Tom in on the script.

"Tom would show up at my house, grab a beer
and we'd work for five or six hours on the
script," said Simpson, who died of a drug over-
dose in 1996. "Sometimes we'd act scenes out.
The guy doesn't see things from just a couple
of perspectives — he can really wrap his arms
around something and see it from all angles.
We had a lot of fun."

The script, from Tom's perspective, had a couple of big problems. One was the love interest, to
be played by Kelly McGillis. Originally conceived
as a gymnast, the trio finally decided she needed
to be more involved in the pilots' world and they
instead made her an instructor at the school. The
second — and bigger — problem was Cruise's
character, Pete "Maverick" Mitchell. Reckless,
cocky, even arrogant as written, the worry was
that audiences wouldn't like him.

The solution? They wrote in some scenes

where Maverick expressed some self-doubts to his flying mate and they gave him a lost father, another pilot who mysteriously was lost over Southeast Asia in the Vietnam War. Whether the plotline came from the recent experience of losing his own estranged father or not, it helped paint Maverick in warmer tones, as a troubled youth needing to prove himself to the world.

"We were out one night in a Spanish restaurant, drinking frozen margaritas," Simpson said, "and Cruise turned and grabbed me by the arm. He leaned over very intense and said, 'You know that scene in the locker room where I'm talking to Goose? I need to apologize to him.' I mean, this is a total non sequitur. I said, 'Tom, I'm looking at the girls.'"

The scene made it into the movie, helping assuage Tom's fears of another bomb.

"I was nervous about *Top Gun*," he said. "I was offered the movie after I made *Legend* and *Legend* was a huge movie and very tiring. After that, I wanted to be careful about getting involved in a kind of epic production again."

"I felt total support from Simpson and Bruckheimer that whatever wasn't right, we were going to make right," he added.

But once on board, he threw himself into the film. He hung out at Miramar, studying planes, studying the pilots. "These guys took one look

at me and said, 'We are going to kick your ass,' "
he laughed.

He also went up in the back of an F-14 — flying
as a "hop" three times in one day. "I flew in the
morning, the afternoon and in the evening, right
before the sun went down," he said. "I couldn't
have asked God for a nicer day to fly. Some
nights, when I can't sleep or I have a lot on my
mind, I just think about those clouds and the
sunset on that afternoon."

Cruise may have been the human star of the
film — but the real stars were the jet fighters.
Half the film consisted of wild aerial footage,
with gut-wrenching 360-degree turns, spins and
rolls. The first scene set the tone: Cruise inches
his upside-down F-14 to within a foot of a Soviet
fighter pilot's cockpit high above the earth and
takes a snapshot of the startled Cold Warrior.

Another star, behind the scenes, was director
Tony Scott. He heard Bruckheimer and Simpson
talking about the concept for the film while on a
rafting trip in Colorado. Scott wanted in so badly
he could taste it. "They were talking about
another director," Scott said. "So I just sat there
drooling. Luckily, it came 'round to me."

But when he got the film, he had to please not
only the producers but Tom Cruise, who was
acting as almost a third producer and who
criticized the first rough cut of the movie.

"The aerial story just didn't work," Cruise said. Scott "had miles and miles of aerial footage. He had to go back and tighten it up, define the story more." Cruise and McGillis also had to return to work after the film was wrapped, to shoot a love scene. Test audiences wanted some skin.

None of the extra work bothered Cruise. "I always try to look at a rough cut like: 'The movie's not out yet — you can fix it,'" he said.

By the time the film was released, *Top Gun* personified the Reagan years of the mid-1980s, celebrating the military and its cocky can-do young men even as other dark, anti-war films such as Oliver Stone's *Platoon* were still mulling over what went wrong in Vietnam.

Top Gun also introduced what was to become a kind of stock character for Cruise — the wounded, ambitious young man with a father problem, seen also in *A Few Good Men*, *Days of Thunder* and even *Rain Man*. Was that just coincidence?

"Well, obviously, my father wasn't a fighter pilot and he didn't die a hero," Cruise said, "but I think a lot of the gut-level, emotional stuff — the love of the father and the conflict in that — is in there."

The film also introduced Cruise to his first bout of controversy, as the film was slammed by some as glorifying war even as it went on to earn an incredible $176 million after its 1986 release. Cruise addressed the issue head-on, saying he had anticipated trouble from some quarters.

"I realized getting into it that the movie was going to get hit from people thinking it was a right-wing military movie," Cruise said. "But what excited me about the film — and I think you have got to approach it by looking at how it's been shot — was the planes. I love planes. I saw the movie as *Star Wars* with real aircraft. What we were reaching for was more of a sense of competition, the old rah-rah military. And then the Navy set up recruiting stands right outside of theaters. I can't control that and I can understand how people would say, 'Well, you are killing people in *Top Gun*.' But I did not make the film as a propaganda movie."

"I mean, if we really wanted to make an all-out war movie with people jumping in their seats, we could have gone a totally different way with it," Cruise told another interviewer. "We could have had MIG battles throughout the whole piece. From the opening straight through the end, there could have been blood and screaming."

Cruise acknowledged that he wasn't necessarily the main attraction in *Top Gun*. "There's always gonna be that fascination with the pilots and flying," he said. "The whole trick about that film was the jets. It was the gimmick that made the film work."

The film made a lot of money, created a lot of buzz and finally established Cruise — who earned $3 million for the role — as the most bankable star in Hollywood second only to Harrison Ford. But *Top Gun* was really just half a movie — though audiences ate up the aerial scenes that seemed to put them in the cockpit, the plotline involving Cruise and McGillis remained on terra firma.

"The simplest way to sum up the movie is to declare the air scenes brilliant and the earth-bound scenes grimly predictable," one reviewer wrote. "This is a movie that comes in two parts: It knows exactly what to do with special effects, but doesn't have a clue as to how two people in love might act and talk and think."

At just 23, Tom Cruise may have needed more life experience to draw on to make his onscreen romances believable. And whether he needed it or not, he was going to get it.

Chapter 7

POOL

'I LIKE BRIGHT, VERY SEXY women," Tom Cruise said in 1986. "And strong — someone whom I'm not going to run over, someone who's going to stand up to me. She's also got to have her own thing going. I don't want someone living for me."

Now that he was *Top Gun*, Cruise was subjected to the Hollywood gossip mill. Reports linked him with Daryl Hannah, the long-legged, blond star of

Splash — which surprised Tom. "I had never met her," he said. "I don't know why people think I'm running around with everybody."

Other reports mentioned McGillis, Lori Singer and even Cher. At least he had met her. "She's funny and bright and we're good buddies and that's it," he protested.

In fact, Tom was seeing someone: actress Mimi Rogers. They met while Tom was absorbed in *Top Gun*.

Mimi was 11 years older than Tom, and had knocked around Hollywood since the 1970s. She had been in a couple of failed television series — *The Rousters* and *Paper Dolls* — and was a great beauty. She'd been married before — to Scientology counselor Jim Rogers — and since then had dated Tom Selleck, *Hill Street Blues'* Ed Marinaro and the Kennedy family's Bobby Shriver.

She came from a similar background as Tom's. Her parents divorced when she was 7 years old, and she and her brother stayed with their father. He moved them almost annually to different cities — Tucson, Washington, D.C., Detroit, Los Angeles, San Francisco. Mimi, like Tom, knew all about being the new kid on the block.

But where Tom, for all intents and purposes, had been an overnight success — "I spent a couple of months as a starving actor," he laughed once — Mimi was the flip side to his meteoric rise. She worked steadily, but like thousands of knockabout actors and actresses in Tinseltown, she was still looking to really make it.

"We met at a dinner party," he said. "There were about 10 people there. She sat right next to me. I thought, 'She's very bright, very sexy, very easy to talk to. We just had a lot in common, including the same sense of humor. We had a lot of laughs."

There was one small complication, however. "She was dating a friend," he said. But within a year, they were an item.

Tom had been linked publicly before to just one woman — Rebecca De Mornay. Now, he said he had never loved Rebecca. "There were girls you like a lot," he said. "But I'd never been in love before." Since falling in love with Mimi, he said, "It's opened me up a lot. I think it's helped me become a better actor. We live a lot of life together. We share everything."

Tom spilled the beans about Mimi in a June 1986 interview, no doubt breaking the hearts of millions of women who had learned to worship him as Maverick. But Tom, the product of a broken home, was leery of marriage.

"I go back and forth," he said at the time. "When you don't feel like getting married, marriage is just a piece of paper saying that two people can own each other. I have a very cynical attitude about it. But then, I look at my sisters, and they're married and happy. I don't know, maybe one day some woman will come along and I'll say, 'Let's do it.' "

Cruise allowed that his parents' experience colored his view of the institution.

"You question the whole structure of marriage," he said. "How do you keep it interesting? How do you keep from thinking, am I just being safe here? Am I growing? I don't know if I could get married. Right now, in my present state of mind, I don't think so. I need a lot of space for myself and my work. But I do enjoy being in a relationship."

Tom and Mimi had time to answer those questions while working through a long-distance romance. Tom had been tapped to star alongside the legendary Paul Newman in an update of Newman's *The Hustler* and was required to be in Chicago for the shoot.

The film dropped into Tom's lap while he was still doing *Top Gun*. Director Martin Scorsese and Newman had been developing the sequel to 1961's *The Hustler* titled *The Color of Money* and, Newman said, never really considered anyone but Cruise for the part of Vince Lauria, the protégé pool hustler.

"I was doing *Top Gun* and I was really tired," Cruise recalled. "I had been involved in the piece for about 10 and a half months, shooting six days a week. I was getting lunch with some friends when I got a call saying, 'Mr. Scorsese would like you to call him.' I had met Marty before, so I called him and he said, 'I've got a script that I'd like you to read.' So I said, 'Terrific. Love that, Mr. Scorsese.' I was really excited. I read it and I thought, there's a role here for me."

By 1987, Scorsese had helmed some of the greatest films of the post-War era, including *Mean Streets, Taxi Driver* and the classic *Raging Bull*. He made films, not movies. Cruise had said he wanted to work with the "best people" to continue to grow his career. Working with Scorsese and Newman would be a dream come true for the young actor.

"If Scorsese hands you a script, I don't know how you couldn't like it," Cruise said. "I couldn't turn down an opportunity to work with Paul and Marty. Just the learning experience. That's why I wanted to work with Coppola, even though I knew it wasn't a great role."

The Color of Money did offer a great role: Cruise would play the heir apparent to the role Newman had plumbed so wonderfully, pool shark Fast Eddie Felsen. Newman played Fast Eddie 25 years on, tutoring Cruise's Vince in the ways of the hustler. Cruise absorbed everything he could from Scorsese and Newman — and he and Newman became fast friends on and off the set.

"He was terrific," Cruise said of Newman. "Very relaxed, extremely bright, well read, obviously a very cultured man. And very unassuming — a real humanitarian, very giving to everyone."

"Being with him is a confirmation that you can have a full life outside work," Cruise added. "I love my work and get so focused and driven sometimes. He's taught me that you've got to love life in order to bring life to the roles you play. He introduced me to [car] racing, which is a great release for me."

Cruise studied Vince, trying to decide how best to play him. "A lot of times, looking at a character, first you decide what they're afraid of," Cruise said. Vince, he decided, "was afraid of being alone, because, in some sense he's always alone. Vincent has a lot of fears — that's why he moves so fast. When you see him walking, it's a skip and a jump."

During filming, Cruise tried new ways to improvise the character. During a scene where Fast Eddie is teaching Vince some of the ropes, Cruise abruptly walked over and hugged Newman. Scorsese said Newman "didn't know what was going on and the expression on his face was perfect."

The Color of Money was released in October 1986 — and was a critical smash. Earnings-wise, however, it was no *Top Gun*, with $52 million in box-office receipts.

"It would be hard to exaggerate the complex pleasure and wonderment that *The Color of Money* conveys," wrote Paul Attanasio in *The Washington Post*. Reviewers raved about Scorsese's direction and Newman's acting. But they didn't forget Cruise, "whose portrait of Vince is big and bold, tempera paint in primary colors," according to one reviewer.

"Cruise knows how to make his props work for him, too — the silly, '50s-style pompadour, the shirt from the toy store he works at with 'VINCE' in big block letters, the playful way he wields the pool cue. He's not afraid to color Vince, to show you how he's vain and impulsive and even a little stupid, because he knows that the gusto with which he dives into the role will wash over everything."

The roles of mentor — Newman — and protégé — Cruise — didn't just exist onscreen. "I think there's an element of that, of the older guy passing on the torch to the younger actor," Scorsese noted.

The words were pure validation for Cruise, whose acting hadn't exactly won an Academy Award in *Top Gun*. He wanted to work with the best people and grow. The raves for *The Color of Money* kept him on track.

"I'm very proud of *The Color of Money*," Cruise said. "But not every movie I make is gonna be a major hit. I can't just do romantic action movies that I think are going to be highly commercial, because you end up doing them for the wrong reasons. And as long as people keep hiring me, I'm gonna take a lot of chances and make some really good movies. And some not very good movies — hopefully, not too many."

Chapter 8

DRINKS

CRUISE WAS WAITING FOR another project, *Rain Man*, to rev up, having originally agreed to do the film in December 1986. Cruise and co-star Dustin Hoffman both badly wanted to do the movie, but endless rewrites and other hassles kept pushing it back.

He decided to take "six or seven months off" while waiting for *Rain Man* to come together. "There were problems with *Rain Man* and there was nothing I really wanted to do," he said. "I'll never do that again. I don't like to stay in one place. I live in New York, but after I'm there for, like, three months, I'm ready to travel somewhere or do something. I like a lot of change."

And make a change he did — in his marital status.

On May 9, 1987, "in a ceremony so secret even his publicist didn't know about it," as one report said, Cruise and Mimi Rogers wed in upstate New York. Tom's old *Outsiders* pal Emilio Estevez, who had just recently broken off an engagement to Demi Moore, was Cruise's best man. Tom's mother Mary Lee called the wedding "very small, intimate and beautiful." Her new daughter-in-law, Mary Lee said, was "top notch. I couldn't be more blessed. Mimi is exactly the kind of woman I always hoped Tom would marry."

Cruise had spent the previous year waxing enthusiastically about Mimi when asked, and to those who questioned the age factor — she was 35, he was 24 — Cruise said it was not even an issue. "I don't think age has anything to do with anything," he said. "You meet someone and it's not even a consideration."

Cruise and Mimi had weathered the distance and the time away from each other and finally had been able to reunite during Tom's hiatus after *The Color of Money*.

What changed his mind about marriage? "Her friendship," Tom said. "Being able to be myself and be 100 percent OK, accepted at every level, good or bad. To have that understanding, and just have someone know everything — it's a relief."

Cruise also found an acting soul mate in Mimi, someone in The Biz. That was important. And perhaps Paul Newman's own example — his successful decades-old marriage to actress Joanne Woodward — had a hand in Cruise's decision to tie the knot.

"To have someone understand that performing's a lot of your life — and to get excited about it, and that's OK," he said. "I always thought, how am I going to find someone, how can I carry on a relationship and work at the same time? That's my life, work. But it's easy. It just fits."

"I never thought I'd marry an actress," he told another interviewer. "I always thought I'd marry someone else. But the thing is, she understands the way I think, the way I work. When I work, I work around the clock. We've arranged it so that she works, then I work. I spend time with her on her sets. And it's fun. For me, it's fun."

Cruise and Mimi kept things low key — so low key, in fact, that the invitations to their wedding mentioned only a "Spring Bash" at the rented estate. But one of his sisters was in on the deal — and baked the wedding cake, chocolate with white marshmallow icing.

"It was just a lot of fun," Cruise said. "We had a few friends there, but basically just family. We were married in the morning at a house I was renting in upstate New York. Everyone stayed for the weekend. It was a warm, wonderful day."

Mimi had just finished *Someone to Watch Over Me*, which co-starred Tom Berenger. The couple had no honeymoon planned, though. Cruise, it was noted, was still awaiting rewrites of *Rain Man*.

His patience finally exhausted, Cruise decided to sneak in a project before *Rain Man*. He agreed to a role as a "star bartender" in what was supposed to be a dark, indie-style commentary on the 1980s — *Cocktail*.

"The character is a dreamer, very optimistic, but he really gets slammed down," Cruise said. "Brian Flanagan, in *Cocktail*, is more of a wannabe, a guy who wants to be a yuppie and he just can't. He wants to be, and he's just not being let in. He wants to be successful in life, and he sacrifices his own ethics. I think this is a movie that really rings true for anyone who's in the singles world or who really wants to be successful. A lot of people assume other people's ways of living and end up destroying themselves."

In the film, Cruise's ambitious character is counseled by the older Doug Coughlin (Bryan

Brown) to latch onto a rich woman to finance his dream of owning his own singles bar. Cruise's Flanagan winds up pouring drinks in Jamaica, falls in love with a vacationing New Yorker, beds another powerful businesswoman and gets caught — but in the end everything turns out OK when the girlfriend turns out to be pregnant AND rich.

Elisabeth Shue, one of Disney's favorite young actresses, was signed on to play Cruise's love interest. The director, Roger Donaldson, expressed high hopes for the film and for Cruise, who earned $3 million for the flick.

"I've always felt that Tom was one of those young actors whose abilities had sort of exceeded the material he had to work with," Donaldson said during the filming of *Cocktail*. "They haven't been in movies where people have said, 'This guy is Oscar material,' know what I mean? That quality that makes him so magnetic to the audience hasn't been exploited in a movie where Tom was taken seriously as an actor. And I think this piece could well do that."

That the film would actually turn out to be an embarrassment for almost all involved wasn't Cruise's fault. He leapt into the role of Brian Flanagan with the same enthusiasm he had shown in *Top Gun* and *The Color of Money*. He attended bartender school with co-star Bryan

Brown and interviewed 34 bartenders throughout Manhattan.

"It's like a war!" Cruise said of a night he spent bartending at a crowded New York gin mill. "People are just all over you. You have to control the crowd — otherwise they'll eat you alive. The end of the night after I worked, I was wired."

Cruise and Brown practiced flipping bottles, wheeling and pouring drinks in a kind of behind-the-bar ballet. They were "new age" bartenders and everyone involved seemed to hope the film would create the same frenzy about bartending that *Top Gun* had produced for fighter pilots.

But in the end, all the bottle-flipping just looked silly, and the plotline left viewers wondering if Cruise really wanted to be a serious actor, or was just chasing the zeitgeist in hopes of a huge payout, a la *Top Gun*.

"After all his noise about serious acting," began a review in *The Washington Post*, "Tom Cruise does Cocktail, the definitive coffee table movie. Think of it as *Top Gun* with drink umbrellas, *Flashdance* with juggling bartenders, *The Graduate* in night school ...

"Cruise is walking in the footsteps of Troy Donahue and John Travolta here. He does what comes easy. He bumps and grinds and grins till his lips ache. It's the performance with the integrity of wax fruit. And *Cocktail* is mud in your eye."

Another reviewer was equally scathing, saying of its ridiculous and mismanaged plot: "The more you think about what really happens in *Cocktail*, the more you realize how empty and fabricated it really is."

The suggestions of a sell-out made Cruise bristle. "I really don't know what is commercial and what is not commercial," he said. "If you look at *Top Gun*, you think, even from the bad script, that it has very good commercial potential. But *Top Gun* could have totally gone the other way. It's got to be a roller-coaster ride and it could have been a kiddie ride. With *Cocktail*, they were nervous about making the picture because it's a character piece and it doesn't jump out at you. It's kind of a stern, serious depiction of what the American dream is now. And the character never really becomes this great success. In the end, what the film says is that 'You have got to be happy with where you are and who you are,' and I don't know if that's a real commercial idea. But then, maybe it's an idea that will generate millions of dollars. It's very hard to tell."

He told another interviewer: "Listen, for me it never has and never will be the money. That's not to say the money isn't great and that I haven't gotten it. But still, I ask myself if I'm going to enjoy what I choose to do."

Cocktail was, despite its many problems with

plot and character, a box-office success, raking in $78 million — proving, if nothing else, that Tom Cruise was a very bankable star — and he was able to laugh off the experience later.

"We made some mistakes with it," Cruise acknowledged. "It wasn't quite the film that we had thought it was going to be. It tended to make critics really angry for some reason. Really angry. Viciously angry. It's interesting."

Told by one writer that the supposedly hip, hip New York bar scene portrayed in the film instead "was filled with clubs and clientele that looked as if they belonged in a shopping mall in Dubuque, Iowa," Cruise laughed and had to agree.

"What were some of the mistakes of that one?" he asked. "Those are some of my secret pains. I never believed I was in New York. It was just not the night scene in New York. You sit there and you go, 'What the hell happened?' " But he defended the film's integrity. "The film was not exploitive," he said. "*Halloween 5* is exploitive. The film meant well, you know? I worked my ass off on that movie. It knocks you out and you learn."

Chapter 9

THE CHURCH

COCKTAIL SHOWED THAT THERE was a chink in the shining armor of America's newest heartthrob. If the critics reacted with anger to the movie, it was because Cruise himself talked in interview after interview about his high ambitions, how he wanted to work with the best people and always continue growing at his craft. *Cocktail* betrayed that vision, showing a Cruise who seemed willing to walk through a role just to reach the money in viewers' pockets.

And there was something else about Tom that encouraged distrust at this point. Like his famous grin, his growing reputation for controlling every aspect of his career and the nagging false rumors of homosexuality that would dog him in years to come, that something else would become part of the mystique of Cruise and seemingly cast a pall over his erstwhile image of Eagle Scout. The something else was his involvement with the Church of Scientology.

Based upon the writings of L. Ron Hubbard — a former science-fiction writer regarded as the embodiment of enlightenment by Scientologists and a ruthless con man by its detractors — Scientology claims its goal is helping individuals solve their problems through self-styled scientific methods.

"Other efforts to help man have tried to solve his problems for him and in this respect Scientology is different," the church's literature says. "Scientology believes that an individual placed in a position where he can increase his abilities, where he can confront life better, where he can identify the factors in his life more easily, is also in a position to solve his own problems and so better his own life."

The goals of Scientology, as stated, had a strong allure for Cruise. Since childhood, he had believed strongly that if he was going to be somebody, he was going to have to do it himself, with no help from outside forces. He never questioned that he could make his own destiny and had done pretty well at the task so far. Certainly, Scientology was something he could get on board with.

In a reflective moment, he discussed how and why he was drawn to Scientology. "I was 26 years old, 27 years old. I mean, I was right in the heat of everything," he said. "I started reading books on it and I thought, 'God, this makes sense.' Scientology means knowing how to know, and I think as an artist, as anyone who's trying to survive in life, you want ... 'How about some tools to help me?' "

But, even as Cruise was entering the church in the late 1980s, its methods of helping "man" were coming under intense fire. A scathing *Time* magazine cover story in 1991 — titled "Scientology: The Thriving Cult of Greed" — alleged numerous abuses, including draining the bank accounts of new recruits, intimidating critics who sought to expose its inner workings, brainwashing adherents and running financial scams to further enrich its coffers.

The church was also accused of running a

cynical campaign to enlist celebrities, who could put a better face on the church and perhaps dull the criticism. And in fact, the church already had a number of high-profile Hollywood celebrities among its membership, including John Travolta, Kirstie Alley, Anne Archer and the late Sonny Bono. Tom's wife, Mimi Rogers, raised in Scientology, had been married to a prominent Scientologist, and has been widely credited with introducing Cruise to the church (though he has denied she led him to it).

Cruise, noted one writer, "was a big fish" for Scientology, which was "not shy about the usefulness of such a celebrity." And Cruise seemed happy to be a shill for the church. He was featured on posters at Scientology centers around the country. Beneath big photos of Tom read the lines, "I'm a Scientologist. Come in and find out why." Given the enormous amount of negative publicity being generated about Scientology, Cruise's involvement in the church seemed fair game for questioners.

It was troubling — here was a man with no evidence of scandal about him, an American icon who could impact the cultural consciousness of an entire country with one film role — consorting with an alleged bunch of liars. In the eyes of some, Scientology was little more

than a cult. His membership in the church, and
the question about whether Cruise was being
influenced by it, begged explanation, whether
he thought it was fair or not.

"It works for me," Cruise told one interviewer.
"It's helped me be more me and do the things I
want to do. I can't tell anybody what their path
to enlightenment is. It's your own adventure.
The whole thing is about self-discovery and
deciding on your own what is real and true for
you."

"It's something that has helped me to be able
to live the kind of life that I'm living and work
toward being the kind of person that I want to
be," he told another writer.

Tom had no patience with the critics of
Scientology, telling a writer who mentioned the
church's bad press: "The articles you've read
have come from an absolute point of mystery
and not knowing. They talk about how this religion dictates people's lives; it's the reverse of
that. It doesn't dictate anything. The whole
thing is not something that's directed toward
dictating; it's actually directed toward concep-
tual thinking and independent ideas."

"You hear things and then you ask someone,
'Well, have you read anything?' " an exasperated
Cruise explained. And the answer was: " 'Well,
no, I saw it on the news.' "

Cruise claimed in one article to have gotten over his dyslexia by using L. Ron Hubbard's Basic Study Manual, which created something of a stir. "Just recently I've found out that I'm not dyslexic," he announced. "I've found a way to study that has overcome that. Now I can learn quickly."

But when one magazine made the focus of its article about the degree to which Tom's connection to Scientology was influencing his life and sent questions in writing to publicist Pat Kingsley, Cruise personally took the offensive. For a person who was not agreeing to an interview on the subject, Tom had a lot to say. Cruise reportedly demanded that the magazine run his written response to the question in its entirety — or not at all.

Asked about his relationship with Scientology head David Miscavige, whether Scientologists regularly visited him on the sets of his films and whether his staff has been "invited" to take Scientology courses, Tom answered in a blistering torrent of denials.

"The reporter's angle is clear," Tom wrote. "The Church of Scientology doesn't run my life or career. By being asked to answer these questions I'm perceived as having to defend my religion or church and having to deny accusations, a false negative impression is created. This is not what

freedom of religion is about. My friends in the
church don't regularly visit me on the set. But so
what if they did? This line of questioning shows
a lack of interest in learning what the Church of
Scientology represents. I shouldn't be subjected
to an inquiry on my religion ... I have heard this
question before, indicating I have 'handlers,' and
find it repulsive."

In an interview about the same time, Cruise
took a more relaxed tone while discussing
Scientology and his relationship to Miscavige.
"Dave is attacked all the time," he said. "It's ludi-
crous. That is really laughable to me, all the
stuff they try to create about this guy who is
really such a decent, good individual."

However, an affidavit was filed in connection
with a libel suit the church filed over *Time*'s 1991
article — in which ultimately *Time* prevailed.
Andre Tabayoyon, former head of security for
the church, claimed that Cruise and Miscavige
had a "special relationship" that entitled Cruise
to perks at the church's desert retreat in
California. "One is a world dominant celebrity,"
Tabayoyon said in his affidavit. "The other is a
young domineering cult leader who seeks to
'clear' the world and to rule it according to
Scientology beliefs and practices."

Tabayoyon claimed that Cruise's special perks
included the use of a $150,000 gym, the use of

a cottage and staff attendants — all at church expense. And on one occasion, he said, Miscavige ordered a pasture at the retreat to be planted with thousands of flowers for Cruise's enjoyment — only to order the flowers ripped out and replaced with grass when Miscavige didn't like the effect.

What's more, Tabayoyon said Cruise took a Scientology "life orientation course" at the retreat. The coursework, Tabayoyon said, was aimed at further getting "clear" — a well-known Scientology term. In a nutshell, he said the work was all part of getting rid of the "thetans" which — according to L. Ron Hubbard and Scientology doctrine — cling to human beings and cause all their ills and are the result of events that occurred 75 million years ago when billions of aliens were placed in volcanoes on earth and blown up with hydrogen bombs to ease overcrowding in the universe.

"Hey, if you want to know about it, then read a book about it and see what it means to you," Cruise said in an interview. "It's curious to me why people want to fixate on it. It has certainly helped me. Very much so. It has helped my spiritual life. I enjoy it. But people try to create this whole thing about how Scientology is controlling my life and my career."

Cruise continued to defend Scientology as a

religion that gave him many answers. But the questions would persist and would continue to color the public's perception of Hollywood's leading man — as would other, probing inquiries into the off-screen life of Cruise.

Chapter 10

RAIN

CRUISE TALKED ABOUT WANTING to have kids with Mimi. "I'd love to have kids," he said. "I used to say, 'I'm never going to get married, this isn't going to happen.' Now I try not to have any preconceived notions about life. I think I'm just trying to make the time. We'll make it happen. I look at Dustin Hoffman and his family. He's got six kids. The secret to making it work? You just bring the kids with you."

In fact, children were on Tom and Mimi's minds as they settled into marriage. Mimi, 11 years Tom's senior, could hear her biological clock rumbling. Tom, despite his talk of waiting for the right time, was on board. Despite the couple's efforts after their May 1987 wedding — they had no success.

Tom privately was all for having children — now. Watching Dustin Hoffman play with his kids and seeing how family-oriented Paul Newman was had impressed him with the importance of having his own brood. He told a friend at the time, "Mimi and I want a family and we can give a child everything in the world — especially a whole lot of love."

Tom and Mimi were open to Plan B — adoption — as well. But through 1988, they continued on their own.

However, there was another baby that demanded Tom's attention in the short run. After years of talking, thinking and dreaming about *Rain Man*, production was under way. Endless rewrites had been done and three directors had come and gone before Barry Levinson wrestled the film under control.

"It was a hard two years," Cruise said of waiting for things to come together for the film. "But every time they'd go through a change, I would talk to Dustin and he'd say, 'Listen. If we want to make this film, we'll make it. Do you want to make this movie, Cruise?' And I would say, 'Like I want air, I want to make this movie.' And he'd say, 'Well, let's just hang in there and stay tight, and we're going to make this film.' "

Once again, Cruise was working with a maestro — Hoffman won an Academy Award for Rico Rizzo in *Midnight Cowboy* when Tom was just 6 years old — and he looked forward with nervous anticipation to the experience.

"I always think: 'What are they going to be like?' " Cruise said of meeting his famous co-stars. "And just in terms of rejection, because I'll be working with them. Hoffman and Newman just make you feel good about yourself and confident in your work."

Hoffman had his own baggage — he was known as the ultimate perfectionist — but Cruise said from their first meeting, Hoffman put him at ease.

"I'd heard all these stories before," Cruise said. "But I think it's been blown out of proportion, kind of heightened by his success, I guess. He's very generous on the set; he was generous the first time we met. I was with my little sister at a Cuban restaurant. She really wanted to meet him and I wanted to meet him. I just went up and introduced myself. He invited us to *Death of a Salesman*. It was sold-out, but he made sure he got us tickets and invited us backstage.

Then we went out for dinner with his whole family. My sister was just blown away."

It was hard to say who had the more difficult role. In the film, Cruise, a high-strung car importer who is stretched to the limit, travels back to his hometown of Cincinnati after his father's death and encounters, and then must deal with, an autistic older brother he never knew he had as they travel cross-country to Los Angeles. Cruise loved the part of Charlie Babbitt, the younger brother, because it was he who had to change during the course of the story.

Hoffman, as the older, autistic Raymond Babbitt, had to play a character who was childlike, unresponsive, someone who had been shut off by his condition into an interior world nothing seemed to penetrate — except Judge Wapner of *The People's Court* and facts and figures about airplane disasters. Raymond was also a savant, having the uncanny ability to count in a split second the number of toothpicks that spill on the floor in one scene — an ability Cruise's character turns to good use when it's time to count cards in a Las Vegas casino.

"I play a character who has shut himself out emotionally from the rest of the world," Cruise noted. "He can't really take responsibility for someone and really care about them. And during the picture ... my business starts to go under. My character imports Lamborghinis and I make a mistake and get ripped off. This character is always five steps ahead and not thinking about what's going on. I mean, it's just move, move, move."

Cruise understood that in the end, his character was as autistic and unable to deal with the real world as was Hoffman's. "I also think a lot of people will begin to see their own autism through these characters," Cruise said. "Outside of people being entertained and walking out and enjoying the picture, they are going to say, 'God, I'm like that.' Or 'I do stuff like that.' "

Cruise met with families of autistics and studied the condition. He said making the movie changed him and made him confront his own "personal autism," which he described as "an emotional response that doesn't coincide with the event at hand. It's like, you get hit, your body takes the shot, but emotionally you're not even there yet for another two weeks. I've learned to be more in the moment. Just to be here. Not tomorrow. Not thinking about what happened yesterday."

Cruise allowed that the part helped free him from being the "emotionally frozen" person he walked into the role as. "I felt that way," he said. "I felt it in my work as an actor. I felt it just as a person."

Though it was Hoffman who would win an

Academy Award for the film, Cruise's reputation was also restored. He wasn't even nominated for an award, but he could feel himself getting closer. Where *Cocktail* threatened to push him down the road to John Travoltadom, *Rain Man* put him back in the saddle.

Critics focused on Hoffman's acting, not surprisingly. The jury was split 50-50 on whether he actually played a convincing autistic — though the Academy of Motion Picture Arts and Sciences obviously thought he had — Hoffman's Raymond Babbitt carried the film, and it lived or died on Hoffman's performance.

"The picture's subject is fairly easy to state," wrote one reviewer. "It's about the transformation that comes over an angry, callous, soulless young man when he spends time with the brother he never knew he had. But stating why this transformation takes place is more difficult. Because Raymond never becomes accessible to us as a character, we're never sure just what Charlie is supposed to have learned from him. The scenes that might have given us some sense of what Charlie sees in his brother are missing."

And Cruise? "On his own, Cruise gives a passable performance," the same reviewer said. "But he can't supply the insight into Charlie that we need."

"Hoffman blows Cruise right off the screen,"

another reviewer noted matter-of-factly. "Likeable as he is, Cruise confuses spunk for performance. It was appropriate next to Kelly McGillis in *Top Gun* and opposite Paul Newman in *The Color of Money*. But next to Hoffman, it becomes something out of a beer commercial. Instead of playing off or with Hoffman ... Cruise tends to play *at* him, flailing and swearing like a spoiled, grounded pilot in *Top Gun II*."

Despite such reviews, the movie was a block-buster, earning $173 million. Cruise was the most bankable movie star in Hollywood and with the success of *Rain Man*, movie projects could get green-lighted just on a whisper that he might sign on. But Cruise again professed high ambitions.

"I could have made another *Top Gun* three, four, five times and made a lot of money," he said. "But I'm not interested in that."

Chapter 11

BORN ON THE THIRD OF JULY

CRUISE NEXT SET HIS sights on another dramatic role, agreeing to play the part of Ron Kovic in *Born on the Fourth of July*.

Kovic, a former Marine, wrote a best-selling memoir about his life and experiences in the Vietnam War — an experience that left him in a wheelchair after a bullet severed his spine. *Born on the Fourth of July*, published in the immediate aftermath of Vietnam in 1976, was a bitter lament for a childhood in which he, like millions of other American boys, had worshipped at the altar of John Wayne's World War II movies. Kovic rushed off to find his own bit of military glory in Vietnam, only to return from Southeast Asia disillusioned and crippled.

The soldier-turned-writer returned from the war and slowly found himself becoming radicalized as he questioned the "why" of what had happened — to him and a generation. He willingly turned himself into a symbol of and a spokesman against the war. His was a story of transformation from a gung-ho Marine who became one of the most eloquent anti-war activists of his generation.

By 1979, Kovic had a screenplay written by the young and relatively unknown Oliver Stone, and Al Pacino agreed to play the part of Ron. Pacino was the hottest actor in the world at that moment, having electrified American culture just a few years before with his portrayal of Michael Corleone in *The Godfather*, and become emblematic of American disillusionment in *Serpico* and *Dog Day Afternoon*. In anticipation of playing Kovic, he grew a mustache to try Kovic's physical characteristics on for size. But the moment Kovic saw Pacino walk through the doors of the Drake Hotel in New York City four days before filming was to begin, he knew the project was doomed. West German financiers for the film dropped out, killing the project.

"I knew my dream was dead, because Al had shaved off the mustache," Kovic remembered. "When he was growing the mustache, at least we had a chance."

Flash forward eight years. Kovic, keeping the dream of turning his book into a film, has met with Charlie Sheen and Sean Penn about the role. Oliver Stone, the director of *Platoon*, is still in his corner, having written the screenplay from the book years before and gone on to direct *Salvador* and *Platoon* while *Born* languished. Stone has suggested Tom Cruise for the role, but Kovic's not interested. He doesn't want to consider anyone who had anything to do with the military-worshipping *Top Gun*. "I was so angry at the idea of *Top Gun* that I didn't want to see it," he said.

But Stone persisted. "Cruise's aggressiveness is what impressed me," said Stone. "I wanted to take his top-dog strength and turn it on its side, to flip it. It's like *Top Gun* goes to war. You're No. 1, you're Mickey Mantle, but what happens when you get blown out of the cockpit?"

He and Cruise shared the same agent, Paula Wagner, and Stone felt Cruise was right for the part — and couldn't have helped thinking what Tom Cruise could do buzz-wise for a film that had been dismissed around Hollywood as "another wheelchair movie" in the wake of the critically acclaimed Vietnam movie *Coming Home* with Jon Voight and Jane Fonda.

"At that time the budget was only $9 million," Cruise acknowledged. "Because I came on board, we got more money to spend on the film and we knew the movie would be made. Even so, Oliver told me he couldn't help feeling nervous the film would fall through again."

Kovic came around, too. One day he looked outside the window of his Los Angeles home to see Tom Cruise by the curb — struggling to pull a wheelchair out of his car. Cruise wheeled up to the house — and Kovic quickly relented, agreeing to allow the young superstar to play him.

"When I first met Cruise, he was very much a mirror image of myself when I went to Vietnam in 1965," Kovic recalled. "I had never really felt that Pacino connected with me as much as Cruise or that he understood what we had been through. I was touched by Cruise. I was touched the way I am from time to time today by kids who were not even born when I was wounded and they have such insight. Cruise understood. It heals something inside of you. It makes you feel like part of the world again. I knew he could do it. I said to myself, 'Everybody in the world knows who he is. So even if he isn't that strong, at least the film and the message against war will get out to the right people.' "

"I had my doubts before he came that day," Kovic told another interviewer. "I wondered if he had the depth to portray me. We had a meeting in my kitchen for several hours, and Tom explained that he really wanted to do this and he was not going to let me down. I was looking at him, saying to myself, 'He's so full of life. He's so sure. He's so representative of America before the war.' I was thinking: He's about to go through this hell and he doesn't even know it."

For Cruise, born July 3, 1962, the part of Ron Kovic would be the most difficult of his career — but his most important. He had been mostly oblivious to the Vietnam War and much of the divisions in the country that came with it in the 1960s and early '70s. At the time, Cruise was a boy and living in Canada while the conflict and its controversies — the peace marches, Kent State, the sit-ins — seemed far away.

"When I came back to the States, I saw young kids arguing in the playground over who had won the Vietnam War," Cruise said. "Some kid was saying, 'We got our asses kicked in Vietnam'; another was saying, 'We won the Vietnam War.' Another kid was asking, 'What was Vietnam?' Even in high school, we really were not educated about it."

He would have to bone up on the era — and he

would have to learn what it was like to be Ron Kovic, who because of his wound had no feeling below his chest. Cruise spent days in a wheelchair, experiencing the difficulties the wheelchair-bound face just trying to live a somewhat normal life. And there were scenes in the film — one in a Mexican bordello, another at the Republican convention, a confrontation with his puerile mother — that would be exceedingly trying for Cruise, both mentally and physically.

"It was very difficult getting up on curbs; it was exhausting," Cruise recalled. "Every day that I was in the chair, I built up different muscles, but I was still tired. It was a big metal chair and it was uncomfortable going around in it."

"We take a lot for granted," Cruise said. "Getting out of bed in the morning, putting our shoes on, running into the shower, washing our hair, running down the stairs. You realize that for someone paralyzed, just tying your shoes is like bench-pressing 250 pounds or like running marathons."

Kovic was often there with Cruise for moral support — and to provide technical know-how. "I remember I was going around with Kovic and I was in the wheelchair," Cruise said. "I went into this high-tech gift shop and this girl comes up to me and says, 'Excuse me, sir, I am sorry, but could you please stop rolling around on our carpet or I'm going to have to ask you to leave.'

I said, 'Why?' She said, 'Your tires are leaving marks.' I could not believe it."

Kovic and Cruise visited Veterans Administration hospitals around the country, where Cruise was mobbed for autographs. "It was painful once I began to research the film," he said. "I met a lot of young people with injuries."

Cruise told another interviewer: "Ron worked with me on the physical aspects of being paralyzed, but he had a hard time remembering what it had been like in the VA hospitals. So I went to different rehab hospitals to interview people. I met a man who'd had a car accident. I asked him what he dreamed about. He said, 'I dream that I'm walking. I dream that I'm dancing or singing, that I can feel my body again.' Then Ron told me he used to dream about walking out of the VA hospital — which became a scene in the film."

Cruise wound up juggling *Rain Man* and *Born on the Fourth of July*. He would shoot scenes for *Rain Man* in the morning, and rehearse for *Born* in the afternoon. It was a hectic pace, but Cruise loved it. When *Rain Man* wrapped, Cruise plunged into *Born* and lost himself in the character of Ron Kovic.

Kovic, moved by Cruise's portrayal, presented the actor with the Bronze Star he had won in Vietnam as a token of his appreciation.

"The only way I could bring him to life was to

take Kovic's soul — and Oliver's soul — and bring my own out," Cruise said. "I wanted to speak for them with this role. I'm not acting that; that's how I feel about it. It was real for me when I was doing it."

While many reviews focused on Stone's controversial vision and technique, Cruise was praised for his effort. "Cruise's work in front of the camera is as ardent as his director's behind," read one typical review. "But Stone doesn't give his actors much room to work. He's too busy filling in all the details himself."

The film was a rite of passage for the earnest 27-year-old star. Like Kovic, his eyes were opened. He almost sounded like a radical — quite a step for the man who played the gung-ho Maverick in *Top Gun*.

"I'm proud of the movie," Cruise said. "It's a film that tells us we can't blindly trust the leaders of this country, that we ourselves must search and find out where we stand and what we believe in."

"I think he became middle-aged making this movie," Stone said of Cruise. "I think he passed out of his youth truly into early middle age. He'll never be the same boy that he was before. He knows too much now."

Chapter 12

THUNDERSTRUCK

TOM CRUISE WAS 27 when *Born on the Fourth of July* arrived in theaters in late 1989. But perhaps there was something to Oliver Stone's assessment of Cruise as being "middle aged" — by all appearances, Cruise was entering a midlife crisis.

By the time *Born* arrived, Cruise should have been walking on air. The picture was well-received by critics and fans, who shelled out

$70 million for "another wheelchair movie." For the first time, Tom took a percentage of the profits instead of a flat fee for doing the film — a gamble that paid dividends when the film turned out to be a hit. And in short order Cruise would find his hold at the top of the Hollywood food chain further strengthened by an Academy Award nomination for the role of Ron Kovic.

He was revving up his next project as well, an ode to racing to be called *Days of Thunder*. Paul Newman had introduced him to racing and while in the middle of some laps at the Daytona International Speedway, where the two had gone to blow off some steam after wrapping *The Color of Money*, the idea of a racing movie came to Cruise. He took the idea to his old *Top Gun* buddies Don Simpson and Jerry Bruckheimer, and they signed on to produce. Legendary screenwriter Robert Towne — *The Godfather, Chinatown* and *Bonnie and Clyde* were among his efforts — agreed to write the script with Cruise's words as his guideline: "I wanted to take an audience for a ride at 200 miles per hour and have them live to tell about it," Cruise waxed enthusiastically. "I wanted to get inside this world where success and failure come week to week."

But Tom had an issue of his own to deal with — he and Mimi had not conceived.

Friends noticed tiny fissures in the relationship

emerging during the filming of *Cocktail*, shortly after Tom's marriage to Mimi. Friends claimed Mimi was upset by the various love scenes in that movie between Cruise and Elisabeth Shue. Further, insiders said, Mimi was upset by the practice Tom's female fans had of shoving their phone numbers into his hand whenever the couple went out in public. "When Mimi and I were dating," Cruise told a friend, "she thought this was cute. After we got married, she decided it was ugly — and all my fault!"

Cruise tried to keep a lid on the troubles, but after *Born* wrapped, things seemed to be turning ugly between Tom and Mimi — even as he continued to sing her praises in interview after interview. "I wouldn't have been able to make it through *Born*, I don't think, without her being there," Cruise said as the film came out. "There were times I was so physically exhausted and the stuff was very emotional. I couldn't imagine being without her or being alone."

In October 1989, the trouble in their marriage went public. One publication reported heated arguments supposedly resolved when he proffered a love note attached to six dozen long-stemmed red roses as a peace offering. But on Jan. 16, 1990, in the middle of the publicity blitz for *Born*, Cruise announced publicly that his marriage was over.

The timing of the announcement was an embarrassment to Cruise, coming as it did "at the same time that he was being quoted in several national publications about its enduring stability," one writer noted. Indeed, in an interview with Cruise dated Jan. 22, 1990, one publication noted that "the Cruise camp says you can ignore those tabloid tales of marital discord."

In the same interview, Cruise gushed about Mimi. "She helps me," he said. "She was there with me whenever she could be on both *Rain Man* and *Born*; yet she's got her own career, which is just as important as mine."

And, even with the breakup a done deal, he talked about how he made it "work."

"It takes a lot of communication," Cruise said. "If you're willing to do that, if you're willing to be honest and work at it, it pays off a hundredfold."

Cruise wound up apologizing to the press for his duplicity and an arranged appearance on *The Arsenio Hall Show* helped him clear the air. Cruise, for a moment, lost control of his public persona and had to eat crow.

Tom was already living the life of a bachelor when news of the divorce hit. He threw a huge party at the Charlotte Motor Speedway to celebrate *Days* and sources said he handed out invitations to crew members and instructed them to hit the city's clubs and bring back the prettiest girls they could find. Insiders said Mimi found out about the party and called Tom to give him hell.

Friends cited the issues of personal and career jealousy, the time apart and the problems in trying to start a family as reasons for the breakup. It turned out that Tom and Mimi had not even spent the 1989 holidays together — even though both of them were in New York on New Year's Eve — and sources said they had a shouting match in early December on the set of *Days of Thunder.*

Even the advice of Tom's racing buddy Paul Newman couldn't stop the runaway car that had become Tom's marriage to Mimi. "Paul told Tom not to do anything rash," a source confided. "He told Tom, 'Time heals all wounds. My wife Joanne and I found that out a long time ago.' " Tom promised to hold off on divorcing Mimi the source said — but things got out of control. "While there have been positive aspects to our marriage there were some issues which could not be resolved," Tom said in his press release.

Although Cruise denied it, there was some speculation that a very large issue in his divorce was another female — a long-legged, red-headed, 23-year-old Australian named Nicole Kidman.

Nicole was raised in an affluent suburb of Sydney and began attending drama school at the age of 10. She earned kudos in the Australian miniseries *Vietnam* and was hailed as that country's answer to Sigourney Weaver. The year before, Kidman had beguiled audiences in *Dead Calm*. Kidman arrived for her reading for *Days of Thunder* in front of Cruise, Bruckheimer, Towne, Simpson and director Tony Scott — and cracked a joke about there being a lot of men in the room. "No one laughed," she said. "So I put on my glasses and got down to work."

The men — all of them — were impressed. Kidman landed the part of Dr. Claire Lewicki in *Days* — and the official story would remain that Cruise and Kidman did not become romantically involved until the filming was almost wrapped.

But Robert Towne remembered sparks flying when Cruise and Kidman first met in 1989 — even before her reading for *Days*. Having seen the Aussie actress in *Dead Calm*, Towne suggested he and Cruise meet with Kidman for dinner. "From the moment they met, it was very easy," Towne said. "No one had trouble talking."

"When I met her, I thought she was incredible," Cruise has said. "My marriage was basically over at that point, but we couldn't do anything, to be very ethical, until it was over."

The film itself took knocks even before it was

released. The presence of Bruckheimer and Simpson didn't go unnoticed and *Days of Thunder* was quickly labeled "*Top Gun* on Wheels." Cruise tried to dodge the moniker. "It's not," he said. "The characters have depth. It's about America and America's sons, really. Cars symbolize to me creative greatness. These drivers are artists. It's not just about going out there and putting your foot on the pedal."

The film cost more than $55 million to make — $9 million of which went to Cruise. Cruise played Cole Trickle, a rookie NASCAR driver who re-examines his life after a near-fatal on-track crash. Robert Duvall signed on to play the crew chief, the mentor figure needed in all Simpson-Bruckheimer-Cruise efforts. Kidman, of course, was the much-needed love interest. The five-month shoot — most of which took place in Charlotte, North Carolina, and Daytona Beach, Florida — was interrupted by weather problems and delays.

Cruise did not do laps for real in the movie, although he was no rookie behind the wheel. Paul Newman showed him some of the ropes of driving NASCAR-style, admonishing Cruise not to be a hero the first time he helped strap Cruise in behind the wheel. But Cruise had a feel and natural talent for racing — "I feel a need for speed," he had said famously in *Top Gun* — and he set a record for a non-certified driver in Charlotte during a test run on location, clocking in at 166 mph at the Charlotte Motor Speedway.

But for the actual filming, "We built this car and put it on a vibrator," director Scott said. "We sent it blasting around the track on a flatbed trailer at 100 miles an hour with Cruise inside it. There were cameras outside, inside, underneath, all over the place."

Insurance policies prevented Cruise from being in any crackup scenes. "They were very careful," he said, "but I did more stuff than just driving around the track. I didn't do the crashes, obviously. But I had my share of stunts."

Cruise was involved up to his eyeballs in the production and post-production. "It's exhilarating," he said. "Because this is the way they used to make movies. John Ford would shoot a film and six weeks later it would be finished. Hitchcock shot *Psycho* in something like 19 or 20 days and four weeks later it was out in theaters."

Unfortunately, all the gimmicks and all the speed couldn't hide the fact that there was not much of a story to tell about Cole Trickle. The film was rushed out to take advantage of the summer movie season and did well, earning $82 million. But, following on the heels of Cruise's terrific turn in *Born on the Fourth of July*, the film left him open to the same old criticism that plagued him after *Cocktail*. Was he only in it for the money?

"*Days of Thunder*," wrote one reviewer, "is an entertaining example of what we might as well call The Tom Cruise Picture, since it assembles most of the same elements that worked in *Top Gun, The Color of Money* and *Cocktail* and runs them through the formula once again." Among the elements that were "beginning to wear out their welcome," said the reviewer, was "the Cruise character, invariably a young and naïve but naturally talented kid who could be the best, if ever he was to tame his rambunctious spirit."

Cruise didn't seem to get the criticism, focusing instead on the importance of doing what he wanted to do and having it be seen by as many people possible.

In fact, he said he'd rather have a commercial hit than a critical success — a view that seemed to cut across the grain of someone who wanted to be a serious actor. But Cruise stood his ground, saying, with a hit movie "I know it's reaching the public."

"I could make smaller films," he said, "but after running in the Olympics, why should I go back to high school? I don't say I'll only do a picture if it has a $32 million budget. I don't read a script for scope. I look for where can this take me? Where are the challenges as an actor, and who can I have an opportunity to work with?"

Chapter 13

NIC

THE DIVORCE, THE HURRIED production of *Days of Thunder* and a string of 13 movies packed into 10 years had taken their toll on Cruise by the time *Days* opened. He took a long-needed break, time to spend with Nicole, time to reflect a little on the hectic decade that brought him to the top, time to consider his next move.

Tom and Nicole didn't wait long before they went public with their romance. However it started, and whether it had a hand in the break-up of Tom's marriage to Mimi, their romance was out in the open by the time the Academy Awards rolled around that spring of 1990.

Tom was in love. Where Mimi Rogers seemed almost to be an unseen accomplice in his life and career, he brought Nicole to the fore, gushing over her and spilling the beans about their relationship in a way he'd never done with Mimi.

"Before Nicole, I was dissatisfied, wanting something more," Tom Cruise once said. "And that's not because of Mimi, either; it was just two people who just weren't meant to work, and it wasn't what I wanted for my life. I think you just go on different paths. But it wasn't Mimi's fault. It's just the way it is."

"My divorce was just something that needed to be done," he told another interviewer. "I think anyone who has been through a divorce can't believe that it's happening to them, whether you come from a divorced family or not. If anything, maybe I had more of an understanding not to berate myself because of it."

He couldn't — wouldn't — slow down for Mimi. She seemed to have gotten caught up in the 10-year plan he laid out in 1980, when he borrowed $850 from his stepfather to go to New York. "The first 10 years, that was it," he said. "Work, work, work.

"And then I met Nic, and it was like, 'Oh, my God,' " Cruise said of working with Nicole on *Days of Thunder*. "It was that special connection when you recognize your soul mate. She is a person who understands. It was as if a whole new life had started for me."

Reading between the lines, one could get the idea that Mimi had been perhaps too clingy for Tom and maybe just not enough of a superstar herself to keep up with her younger and more famous husband. Also, one could get an idea of the jealousies that may have piled up between Tom and Mimi. He said of Nicole: "The thing about Nic is that she has her own career. It challenges me. I like someone who is going to keep the relationship going and make it fun. Someone who's very honest, so there's nothing unsaid."

Unsaid was the issue of children and whether the couple's lack of children led to the split. Rogers, for her part, denied that children were an issue in the divorce.

Rogers also said she sacrificed her career for Tom during the three years they were married. "I was trying to make the marriage work so I made it a greater priority than my career," she acknowledged. "If I had focused more on my career maybe things would have gone faster for me."

But Tom and Nic did things together that he and Mimi never did. "We jump out of planes; we play racquetball; we swim, read books, play cards, go bicycle riding," Cruise said. And before long, they were talking about diving into marriage.

Tom attended the Academy Awards with Nicole, only to find himself losing the Best Actor Oscar for *Born on the Fourth of July* to Daniel Day-Lewis for *My Left Foot*. Cruise claimed to not be too upset by the loss — and in fact seemed to cheer the loudest for the winner.

"It was just exciting to be there that night," he said. "Sitting there next to Anjelica Huston, Jessica Lange, Jessica Tandy, Morgan Freeman — it was exciting."

"I remember getting into the back of the car with Nic and saying that I just didn't feel upset about it," he said. "Maybe I was relieved. I don't know what would have occurred — having that pressure at 27 years old."

In the meantime, Cruise was considering his next move. The critics could say what they like about The Tom Cruise Picture — he was intent on doing what he wanted. The simple fact remained that Cruise movies made money, and a lot of it, and he was a wanted man in Hollywood.

What exactly was his allure? Was it just the smile? The eyes? The way he carried himself? The overall boyish good looks? Everybody had an answer.

"He's protective and strong and still innocent,"

said Cruise's *Rain Man* love interest Valeria Golino. She cited his eyes as his most attractive feature. "Not their color," she said. "His regard — the way he looks with them. They're very alive."

"If he's shaking your hand, he looks you in the eye," said *Days'* cinematographer Ward Russell. "He's very focused."

"He's a great object onscreen," said *New York Times* movie critic Janet Maslin. "The quality he radiates as an object is this healthy, glowing, all-American well-being. When he just gets out there and plays The Handsome Hunk, then he seems redundant to me. The times he has been great are the times that someone uses that healthy, handsome thing of his, yet leaves him wounded and bewildered by it ... A lot of the intelligence of how he comes across comes from his directors, which is, in a way, the real sign of an old-fashioned movie star."

It's hard to believe now, but Cruise in fact met with director Tim Burton for the role of *Edward Scissorhands* before passing on it. The role went to Johnny Depp, instead, and it's hard to picture anyone else doing the film. But it's interesting that Cruise was at least thinking outside the box of The Tom Cruise Picture. Although it seemed that any picture that had Tom Cruise going in was deemed to be a sure-fire hit.

The box-office grosses for Cruise's last six films, from *Top Gun* to *Days of Thunder*, averaged

$105 million — blockbuster territory, each and every time. Every time a male role came up, the first thought that flashed through the eyes of writer, producer and casting agent was Tom Cruise. That included the lead role in *Till There Was You*, which went to Mark Harmon. "Frankly, Cruise isn't even good casting for it," one person connected with the film said. "He's too young. Although I think they'd cast him for *Yentl* if they thought they could get him."

But another film, *Rush*, intrigued him. "Right now I'm looking for another film," Cruise said after *Days* had been released. "I've been looking for a while. We're in the talking stages on that, just waiting to see a script. It's an interesting story." He acknowledged, however, that he was concerned that the role would entail playing a junkie. "It's definitely a concern," he said. "Let's see what they do with the script."

Rush went to Jason Patric after Cruise passed. His decision to forgo the unsympathetic role left him open, again, to accusations that he liked to play it safe, that he didn't want to alienate his fans — that he was only interested in The Tom Cruise Picture. Such talk enraged him.

"If I read a character who had some value and he was gay or a drug addict — and it had some payoff ... then you do it," he said. "It's like, hey, look, you don't know what's gonna happen. Is it going to hurt my career or help it? You can't think in terms of that. See, right now those kinds of things are available to me, but have I read any great scripts where I wanted to do it? I can say right now, 'No, I haven't.' "

Not happy with the script offerings, Cruise took a breather and focused on his new love with Nicole. She brought him home to Australia to meet the folks and by August, Nicole was sporting a $200,000 pear-shaped, diamond engagement ring — which came with $40,000 matching earrings.

By September 1990, they were seriously talking marriage and began scouting locations for their nuptials. They settled on Telluride, Colorado, a playground to the rich and rustic. They rented cars for guests and booked a $2 million, six-bedroom house. The owner, a Chicago businessman, was told "a Hollywood agent was having a party on Christmas Eve," he said.

Tom had to wait, of course, for his divorce from Mimi to become final. And he had to wait for Nicole's schedule to clear, as she was filming *Billy Bathgate* with Tom's old buddy Dustin Hoffman in North Carolina and New York. Tom, however, was ready. Despite the failure of his marriage to Mimi, he wasn't soured on the idea of marrying again.

"I think anyone who has met Nicole would understand," the smitten Cruise told an interviewer. "It was just like nothing that ever occurred before and just because you get divorced that doesn't mean that's it. I was ready, I was really excited."

"Nicole's a one in a million girl and I knew that if I didn't propose to her, I might lose her," Cruise also told a buddy. "Even though marriage didn't work out with Mimi, I love being married. And I know in my heart that Nicole and I are made for each other."

Nicole, for her part, was surprised to find herself just as ready for marriage to Tom. Before she met Tom, "She wasn't that interested in marriage," a friend said. "She's just starting her own career and didn't want to get sidetracked."

But love — and a proposal note that made her swoon — changed her mind.

"My darling Nicole," the note Tom left on her pillow one night read, "I chased you and chased you until you finally caught me. Now will you marry me?"

The answer was a resounding yes.

"I had three very strong relationships before I met Tom, but I was never going to get married," she said. "Never. But he was the most incredible, unusual man I'd ever met. I think in a relationship you have to work at keeping your partner in love with you. You can't just take it for granted. And I knew that was something he wouldn't take for granted."

On Christmas Eve 1990, Tom and Nicole stunned the world by marrying at the Telluride estate they booked months earlier. The log home was filled with flower arrangements that morning, including a willow arbor laced with white lilies and red roses. At sundown, Kidman appeared, wearing a white silk gown and long train, and joined the tuxedoed Tom for the start of a 30-minute ceremony before a judge. They wrote their own vows to each other, and it was very much a family affair as Nicole's sister, Antonia, was her bridesmaid.

Nicole's friend and fellow Australian actress Deborra-Lee Furness said of the ceremony, "Both Tom and Nicole, as well as their families, had tears in their eyes."

Chapter 14

SEMPER FI

CRUISE HATED BEING SEPARATED from Nicole while she filmed *Billy Bathgate* on the East Coast. Now, as they settled into a new $5 million mansion in the Pacific Palisades section of Los Angeles and began life as a married couple, Tom hit on a solution to the time and distance their separate careers created. Offered a romantic period piece called *Far and Away* before they were married, Tom offered his new wife up as the romantic counterpart to his character.

Director Ron Howard, incredibly, had never heard of her — and didn't even know Nicole and Tom were an item! Tom sent Howard a copy of Nicole's starring turn in *Dead Calm* and Howard was sold on her.

Cruise didn't seem worried that starring with his wife in a major film could be fraught with trouble — from critics, from cast and crew, from the director, from a moviegoing public ready for a backlash against Mr. *Days of Thunder*. Cruise wanted to work again and he wanted to be with Nicole — and that was that.

Far and Away was a saga about Irish immigrants coming to America. Cruise earned $13 million plus a percentage of the gross for the role, playing Joseph Donnelly, the optimistic son of a struggling tenant farmer in Ireland, against Nicole's Shannon Christie, the willful daughter of his landlord. Both wind up aboard a ship leaving Ireland and — what else? — slowly fall in love as they make their way through the 1890s' United States.

The film entailed lots of physical action for Cruise — fighting and horseback-riding — and also entailed a romantic trip to Ireland for Cruise and Kidman.

"We had a ball," Cruise said. "I worked hard

and covered a lot of ground each day, but somehow my life was fuller personally and that reflected professionally."

Cruise, for the first time, tried on an accent for the movie. He was tutored by a coach from the County Cork, where his own character was to have come from. "It was one of those things you keep working at until all of a sudden it kicks in," Cruise said. "I wanted to make it subtle and soft, as real as possible. I didn't want it to get in the way of the performance. I was nervous before going over there. I knew people were going to be paying attention to the accent."

Despite their real-life fireworks, the film was no *Nine Weeks*. Cruise and Kidman didn't even kiss for the first hour and 45 minutes of the film. "We hoped that would work for people," Cruise said, "to build up the frustration so that one little kiss became a big thing."

Filming moved from Ireland to Oklahoma before the film was finished. There, during scenes re-creating the Oklahoma land rush, Cruise was filmed doing some serious horseback-riding. Pretending to fly F-14s or drive stock cars was one thing — really riding two-ton horses was another. "I had to learn," Cruise admitted. "Basically I just got on the horse and went as fast as I could ... And don't fall off at 38 miles an hour because it would hurt. I only fell off the horse

"The Outsiders" (1983), directed by Francis Ford Coppola, showcased the talents of many future Hollywood heavyweights, including (from left) Emilio Estevez, Rob Lowe, C. Thomas Howell, Matt Dillon, Ralph Macchio, Patrick Swayze and Tom Cruise.

On the set of "Taps" (1981) with Timothy Hutton (center) and Sean Penn (right), Tom acted with an intensity that impressed his co-stars.

Tom lets Shelley Long do the talking in a scene from "Losin' It" (1983).

What was just one line in the "Risky Business" (1983) script – "Joel dances in underwear through the house" – slid its way into movie history.

"*There's something earnest and virtuous about him that's quite rare.*"
- Rebecca De Mornay

Despite his initial unsuccessful attempt to get Rebecca De Mornay fired from "Risky Business," Tom and the actress quickly hooked up both on and off screen.

Center stage: By the time "All The Right Moves" (1983) hit theaters, Tom had risen to the top of the Hollywood pack.

Shown here with Mia Sara, the actor said he learned valuable lessons while filming the Ridley Scott fantasy "Legend" (1985).

Tom co-starred with Kelly McGillis and a fleet of F-14s in "Top Gun" (1986).

Flying high with "Top Gun," Tom gets a star on the Hollywood Walk of Fame in 1986.

"Paul taught me that you've got to love life in order to bring life to the roles you play."

Tom and first wife Mimi Rogers attend the premiere for "The Color of Money" (1986).

The actor shares the spotlight with his family.

Dustin Hoffman and Tom starred in "Rain Man," which won an Oscar for Best Picture in 1988.

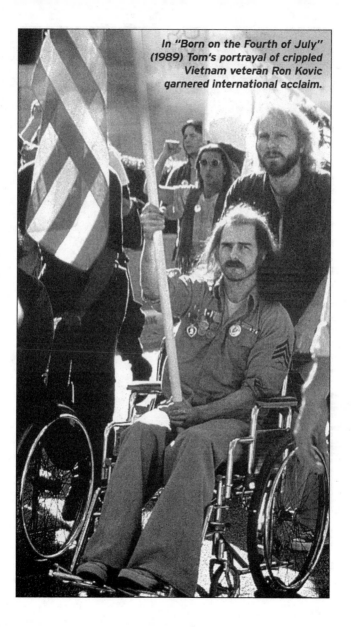

In "Born on the Fourth of July" (1989) Tom's portrayal of crippled Vietnam veteran Ron Kovic garnered international acclaim.

Michelle Pfeiffer and Tom show off their 1990 Golden Globe awards.

Sparks flew on the set when Nicole Kidman played Tom's love interest in "Days of Thunder" (1990) and, once his divorce from Mimi was final, they went public with their romance.

Bruce Willis congratulates pal Tom at Mann's Chinese Theater at a premiere.

Tom interrogated Jack Nicholson in the military courtroom drama, "A Few Good Men" (1992).

"I've never worked so hard on
a character as I did for 'Interview
With the Vampire,'" said Tom of
his role opposite Brad Pitt.

Tom defies gravity by staying at the top of the box-office charts with "Mission: Impossible" (1996).

Tom cozies up to Renee Zellweger (above) in "Jerry Maguire" (1996).

Cuba Gooding Jr. got the film's signature line – "Show me the money!" – and the Oscar for Best Supporting Actor, but viewers came away with a new respect for Tom's acting abilities.

Taking it all in – Tom and Nicole in happier times.

Rolling with fatherhood: Tom gets some exercise with his adopted children, Isabella and Connor.

Tom and Nicole steam up the screen in a scene from "Eyes Wide Shut" (1999) which explored a married couple's sexuality.

In the driver's seat for "Mission: Impossible II" (2000).

"He has that deliciously, indescribable magic that cannot be analyzed or replicated. He is, in every sense, a movie star. The problem is he is such a big movie star that he has to work twice as hard to get you to forget that it's Tom Cruise up there on screen."
- Steven Spielberg

Rosie O'Donnell gets her dream wish – a hug from Tom – but it's while he's being slimed at the Nickelodeon Kids Choice Awards.

Tom strolls through Times Square with new love Penelope Cruz in a scene from "Vanilla Sky" (2001).

"I finished 'Vanilla Sky,' shaved my head and began work on 'Minority Report' the next day."

Tom makes a point with Colin Farrell in "Minority Report" (2002).

Tom Cruise travels the backroads of New Zealand where "The Last Samurai" was filmed.

*Always a professional — Tom helps
a fan snap a souvenir photo.*

*"I do everything I can just to live my
life. You do what you feel is right and
what you know is correct in life and
not worry about everything else."*

once — it was the last shot of the Oklahoma land rush. I fell into a rock pile. We were rushing to do something and I was getting pretty cocky at this point. I'm riding and riding and I just looked down and the horse is full tail and there's dust in front of me and all of a sudden there's a gully. It's too late for me to yank back on him. I just went, 'Oh my gosh!' I fell, flipped back over the horse.

"Nic came up and she was quite frightened and Ron was a little shaken," Cruise reported. "But I have to tell you, it got my adrenaline going."

Coming in at two hours and 20 minutes, the film couldn't sustain the adrenaline of viewers. *Far and Away* was beautifully photographed by cinematographer Mikael Salomon, but relied on what one reviewer called a "sluggish, old-hat script."

There was criticism of the film for its being a "Hallmark card version of life in Ireland" — criticism Cruise rejected. "This isn't *The Field*," he told one interviewer. "This isn't a documentary in terms of what people went through. This movie is not about the Irish. It's about the Americans. It's an adventure and you're either on for the ride or you're not. It's a romantic tale."

There was, reviewers agreed, some romantic magic between the husband-and-wife acting team. One scene, in which Tom says to Nicole, "You're a corker, Shannon, what a corker you are," drew raves from some reviewers. "The delicate sweetness of that moment, magnetically played by Cruise and Kidman," read one critique, "represents the movie at its best. In a summer of impersonal product, this is at least a movie with dreams of more than box office."

Nice try, agreed another critic, but "there's no feeling in it. Howard fails to deliver on both the smaller and larger satisfactions of the form he's attempted; he doesn't give us the sense of the landscape or the people in it.

And the Cruise-Kidman pairing? "Cruise has never seemed more lightweight," the critic said. "As Shannon, Kidman at least brings some ferocity to her performance, even if the character's gumption is of the canned variety. But her forcefulness makes her co-star's work appear all the more paltry."

Far and Away wasn't another one of those Tom Cruise Pictures that annoyed critics, but they gave it lukewarm reviews anyway. And it wasn't a hit, either. It earned a decent $58 million in the United States — Cruise a year later would claim it had earned $130 worldwide — making it his lowest-grossing picture since *All the Right Moves* 10 years before.

Nicole and Tom's relationship, despite the mixed reviews for *Far and Away*, seemed stronger than ever. The couple found themselves well-suited to each other work-wise and every other way. Kidman was an ambitious, hungry young actress. "She had a career in Australia before she met me," Cruise said. "She's a great actress. She works because she's talented. You don't have to know anything about acting or movies to see that one."

"He's just an odd one," Nicole, in turn, told *Vanity Fair*. "He's kind of wild — and I love that. Somebody once told me they were coming back from a rafting trip and Tom was about to go up in one of these choppers. This guy was terrified of choppers, but ... this guy said, 'OK, I'm going to get in the chopper that Tom Cruise gets in, 'cause God isn't going to kill him.' That's kind of what I think, too. He's got that feel about him."

But Cruise — though by no means hungry anymore — didn't spend much time vacationing or taking it easy. Before *Far and Away* was in theaters, Cruise was hard at work on his next film, one which would combine elements of the Tom Cruise Picture with character development and, yes, real acting. Tom would again play a military man — but this time with a twist: He would be a Navy lawyer called upon to investigate the death of a U.S. Marine private in *A Few Good Men*.

Though he received top billing — not to mention $10 million plus a cut of the profits — Cruise didn't have to carry the picture alone. He had the benefit of a strong, high-powered cast, which included Cruise's boyhood idol Jack Nicholson, Kevin Bacon and Kiefer Sutherland. Demi Moore was also cast — but not, strictly speaking, as a love interest. She was there instead to balance out the testosterone and play mother hen and to provide a conscience to Cruise's conflicted Lt. Daniel Alistair Kaffee, a Navy lawyer right out of Harvard.

The story, an adaptation of *West Wing* creator Aaron Sorkin's theatrical play, revolved around Cruise's Lt. Kaffee and Nicholson's Col. Nathan R. Jessup, U.S. Marine commander at Guantanamo Bay in Cuba. Cruise's character is assigned to defend two Marines accused of hazing and unintentionally killing a weaker Marine at the base — and the movie leads inexorably to a courtroom confrontation between Cruise and Nicholson in which Nicholson famously yells, "You can't handle the truth!" and proudly takes responsibility for ordering the "code red" on the dead Marine.

For Nicholson, the role was not huge — but the character was. Nicholson's reading of Col. Jessup was "vicious, funny, superbly reptilian," in the words of one writer. And Nicholson showed up for the first read-through of the script ready to rock and roll all over Tom Cruise's Lt. Kaffee.

"Normally, in those situations, actors are just marking themselves because they haven't yet found all the colors of their characters," recalled director Rob Reiner. "But Jack came in with a full-blown performance that made everybody sit up."

Cruise, Reiner said, stayed with his boyhood idol. "Tom was right there with him, step for step," he said. "He was prepared just as well as Jack, like the young titan and the older titan going at each other."

Cruise gave the credit for being able to go toe-to-toe with Nicholson to being "more in command of what I'm doing," even compared to his earlier work with the equally legendary Dustin Hoffman and Paul Newman. But the nature of the movie helped as well, he said.

"We had great scenes for actors," he said. "I mean, any actor would die to be able to say that kind of dialogue. Even Jack said, 'Boy, these are great scenes to play.'"

As filming progressed, word of Nicholson's hard-assed, menacing turn as Jessup spread around Hollywood and there was a clamor among other Hollywood elite to watch Nicholson work. Cruise, already there, understood the interest.

"He's very unpretentious," Cruise said of Nicholson. "He knows acting and he loves acting. He was really generous off-camera when I was working. He was right there. He'd listen to what Rob had to say and you could see him getting in and trying different things, really hitting his stride and making it sing."

A Few Good Men was a huge hit — re-establishing Cruise as a hit machine. The film earned $141 million — the biggest box office for Cruise since *Rain Man*.

And Cruise finally got his "ideal scene" of a commercial and critical hit. Critics were blown away by Nicholson, but also gave Cruise, Moore, Kevin Bacon and the other actors high marks. Cruise, one writer noted, "takes charge of his central role admirably. But as the scowling Goliath, his lips contorted thinner than a Marine sword blade, Nicholson crushes all opposition."

Nicholson, all agreed, elevated the film. "Nicholson doesn't steal the film, which would mean that he somehow separates himself from everybody else in it," said one reviewer. "Rather, in the course of only a handful of scenes, he seems to suffuse the entire production, giving it a weight, density and point that might not otherwise be apparent."

Chapter 15

MORE HARDBALL

CRUISE DEMONSTRATED THE GOOD sense to step aside and let Jack Nicholson chew up the scenery in *A Few Good Men*. Though he'd gone toe-to-toe with Nicholson in that picture's electrifying courtroom scene, there was no way he could compete with Nicholson's majestic performance, and he knew it. His own work had been good, but once again he was playing the ingénue, the earnest young man who overcomes a father problem and his own self-doubt and triumphs over evil. He was that in *Top Gun, Days of Thunder* and now in *A Few Good Men.* The lack of stretch in his roles left him open to the criticism that he was nothing but an empty suit, a pretty boy, a smile.

False rumors popped up along with that characterization. They never made their way into print or into the airwaves, but they were there, buzzing under the cultural radar. These false rumors had it that Cruise was gay, that his marriage to Nicole was a sham. The talk went hand-in-hand with the false rumors that Cruise was being manipulated by the Church of Scientology, that he was, in effect, some sort of zombie for the church, like one of those pod people in *Invasion of the Body Snatchers.* The talk about Cruise was dark, sinister. It wasn't enough to make people stop going to his movies in record numbers. But it was enough to make people wonder ...

There was nothing Cruise could really do to counter the talk — but that doesn't mean he didn't try. In fact, Cruise approached the trouble with an iron fist and sought to regain control of his image with tactics that only seemed to make the nagging false rumors even more troublesome.

The control began in earnest with the press junket for *Far and Away*. Reporters signing up for mass interviews with Tom and Nicole discovered that they were required to sign contracts stipulating when, and in which publication, their stories would run. The contracts also demanded that writers use the interview with Cruise and Kidman only in relation to their stories on *Far and Away*. "In other words," noted writer Rod Lurie, "the content of the interviews would be the sole property of Cruise."

The junket for *A Few Good Men* went the same way. Kingsley even went the extra mile of trying to make the studio, Columbia Pictures, put the contracts with the media on its letterhead. The tactic eventually would become more heavy-handed, as Cruise and Kingsley asked for videotape of interviews after broadcast outlets had used them and, in the case of CNN, demanded that he be allowed to review previous tapes of its interviewer before he would agree to talk. "Every time we interview this guy," said one exasperated broadcast producer, "we get dozens of calls on signing contracts with him."

But Cruise couldn't make the false rumors about his sexuality and his marriages go away and finally had to address them. Where could they have started? The photo shoot he naively did as a 17-year-old struggling actor in New York? The underwear scene in *Risky Business*? The same place all urban folklore comes from?

By the mid-1990s, they were as firm a fixture to the name Tom Cruise as was Scientology.

The talk certainly didn't die down when Tom and Nicole decided they were going to start a family. Two years after their marriage, the couple filed adoption papers in Palm Beach County, Florida, declaring their intention to adopt a baby. The couple decided on a Florida adoption, said a source, because under that state's law a birth mother couldn't change her mind once she handed over the child.

Tom and Nicole were set to adopt a baby born the day after Christmas 1992 — but their plans were dashed when made public. "They are fearful that the birth mother's identity will be discovered and they cannot deal with the repercussions," Cruise's attorney wrote to a Palm Beach County judge in the course of demanding an investigation into the couple's leaked plans.

The couple quickly recovered from their disappointment when a baby girl born in mid-January 1993 was handed over to them for adoption. Tom and Nicole were overjoyed. "In 20 years of working with adoptions, I have never seen anyone so overjoyed as Nicole was when she first held her new daughter," said a nurse who had cared for the baby. "There were tears of happiness in her eyes as she held the child close to her. It's a blessing from heaven that this baby has been brought together with such wonderful parents."

The ecstatic parents named their adoptive daughter Isabella Jane Kidman Cruise and Tom, already working on his next film in Memphis, Tennessee, spent several weeks at home with Nicole and the baby.

Even before the ink was dry on the adoption, however, tongues were once again wagging. Press reports mentioned over and over that Tom's marriage to Mimi Rogers had floundered at least in part because they didn't have children — and there were questions as to why Tom and Nicole had so quickly decided to adopt, rather than have their own child.

Nicole, bristling at questions about their adoption, said: "I don't want to get into that. Some things are personal. We adopted Isabella because she was meant for us."

"I'd like to give birth," Nicole added. "And adopt more children. We plan to do that. Definitely."

"We talked about children from time to time, but there was always the work," Cruise told *Vanity Fair*. "But then we went, 'When is it ever going to be the right time?' That's how the conversation started. You're lying in bed at night and you're trying to sleep, so you roll over and you go, 'What would it be like if we had this in our life?' "

"Now suddenly we're a family," he added.

Cruise, for his part, saw no difference between fathering an adoptive child and fathering his own biological child. He fell in love with his daughter from the moment he saw her. He said he and Nicole would "one day" have their own children. "It depends on Nic," he said. "We keep talking about four or five kids. But, I don't know. Maybe just two. Who knows what'll happen, you know?"

But in the meantime, he corrected anyone who characterized his daughter Isabella — as well as the son, Connor, he and Nicole later adopted — as not being his own: "These are my children," he said. "These are my own kids. Without question."

But the talk persisted.

The talk might have gone away had Tom and Nicole had their own biological child. But the adoption just deepened the mystery of Tom Cruise to those to whom such things mattered. And Cruise — who otherwise was walking on air at being a father — found himself still angrily fending off the tongue-waggers who prattled on.

"You know what I say about that — basically, that it's attacking my relationship," he told one interviewer. "It is hard-line cynicism and I think it's absolutely disgusting that someone would say it.

"It's ridiculous, it f***ing pisses me off. Personally, I have nothing against that at all, but this is my relationship and I'm being called a liar about it. I've called lawyers. I say: 'You want to say that? Fine, go ahead, you f***ing prove it.' "

It's hard to believe his passionate defense of his relationship with Nicole was an act. And it was ridiculous to believe that a couple would go so far as to adopt not one, but two, children, all as part of some coverup.

But Cruise would never fully control the gossip. He had his fans — but he obviously had his detractors as well. Much of the talk seemed to originate with his association with Scientology, a breeding ground for wild, paranoid rumors both with its followers and its enemies.

Cruise would later develop his own tactic for attacking The Talk. But for the moment, he retreated into the bosom of his family for solace.

"Look at all the stuff that I've heard about myself," he said. "That I'm a misogynist. I'm a homosexual. I'm brainless. How can I be all of those things? So you've just got to go: 'Hey! What the f**k!' Sometimes I'll turn to Nic and say, 'Let's just live our lives and keep doing what we're doing' ... I could spend my time going around saying that's not true and that's not true and that's not true. But I've got so much stuff going on in my life that I'd rather spend the morning with my daughter and my wife and taking care of work."

"Seeing Nicole with Isabella," he told *Vanity*

Fair, "I see a whole other side to her. Sometimes I just stand back and watch. Or I walk up the stairs and just stand there and listen to them play. Sometimes Nic will forget to turn that little baby-speaker thing off, and I'll just sit there and listen to them. Those are the little moments in life when you stop and think, 'I want to make sure I remember this forever.'"

If the actor uttering those words was, in fact, trapped in a sham marriage for the sake of his image and career, he certainly deserved an Oscar for the performance.

Chapter 16

BLOOD

DESPITE HIS CONTENTMENT WITH his beautiful wife, idyllic marriage and family, Tom Cruise was still looking for an Oscar. "Oh man," he told an interviewer, "I think any actor wants to win an Oscar. I'd love to win an Oscar. Honestly, I think it would just be great fun. As a kid you become an actor and it's something you think about. It's like winning the Super Bowl."

But as long as he continued to choose projects that traded any real stretching for mass appeal — not to mention very large dollar signs — Cruise had to content himself with fame and money. And his next project found Tom Cruise playing, once again, the earnest young man who, yes, overcomes self-doubt to conquer the forces of evil around him.

The Firm paired America's hottest actor, Tom Cruise, with America's hottest writer, John Grisham. Grisham, a former lawyer, was making a mint churning out attorney-centered thrillers such as *The Client*.

Though based on Grisham's book, the movie was, in effect, another Tom Cruise Picture, albeit with a nice paranoid twist. The movie, set and filmed in Memphis, featured Cruise as a poor boy who makes his way through Harvard Law School, and gets a whopper of an offer from a law firm that seems on the up-and-up. In reality, as Tom's Mitch McDeere finds out almost too late, the firm is acting as bagman to a variety of thieves and money-launderers, and McDeere finds his own life in danger when he tries to do — what else? — the right thing.

The filming was uneventful — but controversy erupted when one of the film's minor stars ripped Cruise after the picture wrapped. Karina Lombard, who played a hooker hired by the firm to seduce and compromise Cruise's character, portrayed Cruise as a distant and chilly mega-star caught up in the "celeb trip."

Karina told one interviewer, "It would have been nice to exchange a few words, actor-to-actor, before we had to roll around in the sand together, but Tom was surrounded constantly by people."

Others claimed Nicole hovered over Tom during the shoot — mimicking Tom's own behavior while on the set of her film *My Life* in Chicago shortly before. "He was on location every day," a *My Life* insider said. "He sat outside her trailer — preventing anyone from going up to her. He escorted her to the set and escorted her back."

Lombard paid the price for telling tales out of school on the mega-star. Cruise control was exerted on the studio and Lombard was ordered to clam up, according to sources. Sexy publicity shots of Cruise and Lombard were nixed — "which is odd," said a *Firm* insider, "because it's the sex scene in the book on which the movie is based. Those scenes are supposed to be so hot; you'd think they'd use them to hype the movie."

To Cruise, the brouhaha was just more of the same talk. "I've heard everything from I've cheated on my wife to my wife was there on the set of *The Firm* because she was pissed off about my love scene on the beach," he said. "It's not true."

The Firm was unusually long for a Hollywood

release — 153 minutes — but still clocked in with decent reviews. At first glance, one reviewer wrote, "*The Firm* looks like just another variation on Cruise's patented young hotshot roles of the past decade." But the critic added, "The role is an opportunity to sum up his old roles and transcend them with his most potently emotional work."

Another reviewer gave better than so-so marks to *The Firm* and said of Cruise: "One look at Cruise and we feel comfortable, because he embodies sincerity." But the review noted, "He is also, in many of his roles, just a little slow to catch on; his characters seem to trust people too easily, and so it's convincing when he swallows the firm's pitches and pep talks."

Cruise had "grown substantially as an actor," one writer noted. Whether it was his exposure to the genius of Jack Nicholson and other mentors such as Paul Newman and Dustin Hoffman, or simply growth and maturity on Cruise's part, he was bringing new depth to his roles.

The actor felt the growth himself — and with great confidence jumped into a role that would be his ultimate stretch, as well as the source of huge controversy.

The $50 million film was *Interview with the Vampire*, based upon the books of Anne Rice. The role was Lestat — an 18th-century bloodsucking yet very civil, lascivious but gracious vampire. The book and film seethed with homo-eroticism, centering on Lestat's relationship with his beautiful male companion Louis — played by the equally hunky Brad Pitt. The lonely Lestat, smitten with Louis, turns him into a vampire — and later they transform a little girl named Claudia (Kirsten Dunst) into a vampire so they can be a family.

Considering the false rumors that had plagued him, taking on a character that was at the least bisexual was a brave move for Cruise. But he claimed not to care. "This is the way I feel about the homoerotic issue," said Cruise. "I don't care either way. It's nothing I worry about. I'm an actor and I play a character. I do find it a very sensual movie, because everything that Lestat does he does out of love and longing — yet he's sadistic. Lestat certainly loves Louis. He wants a compan-ion. And Louis is beautiful; Lestat finds him so. But, also, Lestat created this creature that Louis has become, so he is very fatherly about it."

To his credit, the role was about as far as Cruise could get from Maverick Mitchell and his counterpart Cole Trickle. Cruise was enthused about the project and looking forward to stretching his abilities, to actually playing a quasi-villain for once.

"By now," one writer noted, "that earnest-

young-man role he has played to perfection seems
to be wearing a little thin. It's become a rather
tiresome routine: The cocky youth matures to
manhood over the course of a 90-minute movie
(applause and roll credits, please)." With Lestat,
the writer noted, "Cruise is entering the dangerous realm of character depiction ... In taking on
the part, Cruise is playing a villain for the first
time in his life — a shallow mass murderer, no
less, an after-hours fiend who sinks his teeth into
every man, woman and child he meets."

Novelist Rice was outraged. *Interview* was
offered to John Travolta, Jeremy Irons and
Daniel Day-Lewis — all passed. The script went
through more than a dozen re-writes in the 17
years since the novel was published, finally
settling back with Rice, who churned out a work-
able screenplay and was to earn $2 million for
her effort, not to mention the increased sales of
her *Vampire* series once the movie was released.
Considering the years and frustrations involved,
one would have thought she'd be happy to have
Bugs Bunny play the role of Lestat.

Rice did model Lestat after an actor, but it
sure wasn't Tom Cruise. She actually had Rutger
Hauer in mind when she created Lestat and she
crowed loudly when Cruise got involved in the
project. Responding to a groundswell from her
loyal fans, Rice blasted Cruise's involvement in

the picture, saying the actor was "too short" and his voice was "too high." Tom Cruise playing Lestat, she summed up, was like Edward G. Robinson playing Rhett Butler.

She later claimed she was making a fuss for her fans. "These people have stood in line for me for three or four hours," she said. "They are my readers and they hate this. I was carried along by my readers. I didn't start the whole thing at all."

Interview producer David Geffen blasted right back. "People are such fools when it comes to these kinds of issues," he said. "If you let fans make the movies, as opposed to the people who make them, then you wouldn't have ended up with *The Godfather* because Al Pacino was just this thin little guy. So it doesn't matter. It doesn't bother me. The only thing that bothered me about people's reaction to Tom was that I know how sensitive Tom is and I knew that it would hurt his feelings."

For Cruise, it was indeed a hurtful, confusing catch-22. He'd been blasted by critics for years for not taking enough chances — and now that he was making the biggest gamble of his career, he was catching more flak than ever.

"When it first hit, it really hurt my feelings, to be candid about it," Cruise said about the criticism. But he credited Kidman with helping him tune out the negative blather. "Nic makes sure I don't go off into space," he said. "When you're under that much pressure, you have to be able to say, 'OK, this is outrageous. I'm going to get slaughtered. But I'm going to do it.'"

The controversy finally blew over without a change of actors and Cruise went about the business of preparing for the role. "Before we started *Interview with the Vampire*, I wanted to see Paris," Cruise said. He and Nicole "went over and walked through all these beautiful old homes and museums."

He visited Versailles. He went on a diet-and-exercise regimen and lost 12 pounds, the better to reflect the vampire Lestat's wasted physique. He grew his hair long and streaked it blond. "I don't know how this movie will turn out," he said during filming. "All I know is as an actor I'm having a great time playing this character."

But there were other problems to deal with during filming. Tom clashed with his co-star, the then-up-and-coming Brad Pitt, who played Louis, one of Lestat's vampire companions. After the film wrapped, Pitt said he and Cruise did not get along during the shoot.

"He bugged me," Pitt said. "There came a point during the filming when I started really resenting him. I hated doing this movie. He's North Pole, I'm South. He's always coming at you with a handshake, where I may bump into you. There was this underlying competition that got in the way of any real conversation."

Interview director Neil Jordan confirmed the tension between Cruise and Pitt. "They're very different," he said. "They have two completely different approaches to life. Brad is all emotion. Tom plays all aggressive, an individual who's all icy.

"In the movie, Tom's character loves to be in control and loves inflicting pain on Brad's character. In many ways they behaved to each other the way their characters did."

A source on the set said things went downhill from the first day, when Cruise realized that 6-foot-tall Pitt was towering four inches over him. "Things were never really smooth. Tom and Brad are both Hollywood pretty boys and don't like to share the bill with other male stars. Tom was feeling insecure. He's always had this reputation as a sex symbol, but here he was up against this real strapping hunk of a man. He didn't like it one bit."

For the second time, an actor had broken Hollywood's unwritten rule about not dissing other actors by kvetching about Cruise's cold, impersonal manner. Karina Lombard had done it after *The Firm* and who ever heard of her again? But Pitt was another matter. He was in line to challenge Cruise's throne as the top Hollywood hunk and had the power to speak his mind without worry of repercussions from Cruise & Co.

The turmoil didn't die with the release of the movie. Cruise's leap was appreciated by some critics, while others declared him flat-out wrong for the role.

"Give Cruise credit for guts," wrote *Rolling Stone*. "It's an audacious performance. He broke ranks with the bland before in *Risky Business*, *Rain Man* and *Born on the Fourth of July*, but *Interview* is a real bust-out. Any star willing to kill women, children and pets onscreen is not that worried about protecting his image."

"His performance pulsates with that hyper-motivated pep many find appealing, but he just ain't The One," countered the *Washington Post*. "Picture *Blade Runner* replicant Rutger Hauer, picture Nazi commandant Ralph Fiennes, picture really big guy John Goodman before you picture Cruise."

Interview with the Vampire was a commercial success, raking in $105 million, and Cruise had to be pleased with his work. The film had been something of a mission impossible, what with all the turmoil and controversy, and yet he had overcome it all and made a film that was both a critical and financial hit.

After all was said and done, Cruise was pleased with his stretch. "I've never worked so hard on a character as I did for *Interview with the Vampire*," he said. "I lost 18 pounds. I worked on my diction, my movement. I read out loud from classics so that the language became easy for me. I was nervous about it. But it was the fear that drove me into it. I've always had this thing that when I was afraid I never backed off. I always went forward."

Chapter 17

DADDY

THE CRUISE-KIDMAN BROOD grew by one following Tom's work on *Interview* when, two years after adopting Isabella, Tom and Nicole arranged for another adoption, this time a newborn boy they named Connor.

The baby, if it mattered to anyone, was black. Cruise would not discuss the adoption, except to say: "That's his story and our story together, and I don't want our relationship — and the same goes for Isabella — to be defined before he can define it himself. And if he wants to tell his story when he grows up, you know, he'll tell his story."

Reports had the couple ready and willing to adopt at least six children — but Kidman wasn't so sure. With two babies, and despite the presence of a full-time nanny, "We're both exhausted," Kidman said. "If we adopt more or of if I give birth to a child — which I'd love to do — it'd be when we can give them the most love we can give. Right now, our hands are full. Maybe that will be different in five years, but right now we're trying to give them their own time so that they have their mommy and daddy and the attention they deserve. Right now, I'm not capable of anything more."

"I just want to make sure we can give the kids the attention," echoed Cruise. "You start getting four kids, it starts to ... it remains a problem through the years."

But adopting children had allowed Cruise to have an epiphany, of sorts. Changing diapers for the first time, he said, "I was scared to death! I didn't know what the hell I was doing!" And running after toddlers had given him a new appreciation of his own parents and his own mortality. "I remember when I used to go out and party all night and sleep in till noon or 1 o'clock," he said. "Now 9:30 seems decadent."

And being a father taught him something

about Tom Cruise Mapother III — that despite the estrangement and troubles in his youth, he realized, maybe for the first time, that his father truly loved him.

"I think sometimes what it would have been like for him to see me with my daughter," he said. "When I look at Isabella, I finally realize that there is no possible way that a parent can't love their child."

"It's given me a greater appreciation for them," Cruise said of his parents. "For their mistakes and for what they accomplished. In today's day and age, everybody blames their parents, but I believe you've got to take responsibility for yourself. Being a dad has given me an understanding that everybody did the best that they could."

Cruise had money, a beautiful wife and, finally, his own family. "One of the things that Nic and I talk about is that now suddenly we're a family," he said. "We're at that point where we're trying to define where we are. Are we really boring? Oh, my God ... we're old!"

Kidman, for her part, had finally scored a leading role. Cruise, Kidman and Isabella headed to Toronto following the filming of *Interview*, where Nicole starred in *To Die For*, a role she snatched from the clutches of Jodie Foster, Holly Hunter, Bridget Fonda and Patricia Arquette. "Tom and I have been alternating films," she said, "though we never actually sat down and worked it out that way. So I owe him one."

Cruise brought Isabella by the set every day for lunch and then headed to the zoo or a park for the afternoon. "He was there the whole time I was doing the film," Nicole said. "People would say to me, 'Oh, you're so lucky that he's here and would do that for you,' but this is the '90s. It's about being a good father. Tom does it because he wants to do it."

"I love spending time with my kids," he said. "I derive incredible pleasure from being a husband and a daddy. My family is the most important thing in my life."

When *To Die For* wrapped — and Nicole would get fantastic reviews for her turn as a murderous adulterer — Tom's turn came in the form of a mission impossible — literally. Based upon the 1960s TV show about a team of intelligence agents who perform high-tech and improbable — but never impossible — missions to keep the world safe for democracy, *Mission: Impossible* brought Cruise back into the action-hero arena.

This time around, Cruise was the producer as well as the star. He spent days sweating over the script, the locations, the cast and crew, at his production company, headquartered in a plush suite of offices that once housed Howard Hughes' production facilities. Producing was a big step forward for Cruise, but he gladly accepted the responsibility for the $64 million production.

It was also another step forward in taking control — though Cruise deflected that reasoning. "It's not really about control," he said. "After all the pictures I've made, I've learned how to do things efficiently. When I first started as an actor, I always knew that one day I wanted to produce my own movies and direct. It just comes down to loving movies."

Cruise said he felt "like a kid in a candy shop" producing *Mission*. He left the early drafts of a script to director Brian De Palma and *Schindler's List* screenwriter Steve Zaillian. They worked from scratch — "six weeks, every day," said De Palma — and then brought in David Koepp of *Jurassic Park* screenwriting fame when Zaillian left for another commitment. When Koepp had to split, Cruise brought in famed script doctor Robert Towne, with whom he had worked on *Days of Thunder*.

Meanwhile, locations were scouted and secured in Prague, London and Virginia, and an international cast including Vanessa Redgrave, Jon Voight and Emmanuelle Beart were signed. It was, Cruise said, "a big, big movie."

Cruise deferred a salary, taking a percentage of profits instead. Cruise put up $20 million of his own money to help fund the production. He told De Palma, "I've thrown in my $20 million, you'd better throw in yours," meaning he wanted De Palma to keep expenses down on the film.

There was pressure on everyone — Cruise, as first-time producer, and De Palma, who had bombed with *Bonfire of the Vanities* and other films since scoring with *The Untouchables*.

"There was a lot of pressure on us because, like anything, you have to prove yourself," said Cruise's longtime agent Paula Wagner.

"Tom was really under the gun with this picture," said Towne. "It was the kind that could have gone over $100 million just by batting your eyelashes the wrong way. We were working in countries where the governments and civil service were barely under control, with a script that wasn't finished and a lot of high-tech s**t to shoot. It was a lot to handle."

Added De Palma: "You're going in with this huge movie star who wanted to make an action picture."

But there were problems right away. On location in Prague, the company found itself being gouged by the Czechs. "Prague ripped us off," Cruise said. "They're still getting used to democracy. But we also made some mistakes with our negotiations that we have to take responsibility for."

The early and rising costs created friction between Cruise and De Palma, but Cruise characteristically downplayed any problems. "How can you make a movie and not have arguments?" Cruise said. "You're with this person every day, it's very tense, there's a lot of money at stake and you get tired." But he said he had a responsibility "to let De Palma know the movie had to be made for a price. You've got to get to the point where all the social bulls**t goes away and it's like, 'OK, you and I are out for the same thing here, so let's get down to it.' It was fun, and it was all to make the movie better."

But, Cruise said, "It was never, 'I'm not showing up' or 'I'm not doing this.' Or Brian putting his hands up and going, 'F**k you, I'm outta here.' "

Still, there was "no shortage of opinions on this movie," said David Koepp. "No one was going to roll over and let the other's creative opinion rule the day. We all have egos."

Tom, Nicole and the kids moved to London and Prague, where they stayed at the Hotel Praha. They entered and exited through the delivery entrance for privacy — even in Eastern Europe, Tom Cruise was a movie star. The hotel went out of its way to accommodate the famous star and his family, having murals of fairytale characters painted on the walls of the children's room.

Not so accommodating were the police. At the end of one tough scene, Cruise was headed back to his trailer, only to be stopped by a Czech cop who demanded his "papers."

"He was speaking in Czech," Cruise said. "I said, 'My papers? What do you mean my papers? We're in Prague, you know. Communism is about two miles back, pal.' " Cruise wound up sitting in a police car while a supervisor was rounded up. "He was just being a bully," Cruise said of the cop who detained him. "But it was like 'What else can happen?' "

But not everything was a hassle. Tom and Nicole took occasional strolls around Prague and on one occasion headed out for dinner and invited their limo driver, Tomas Charvat, along. "I left them alone," Charvat said. "I realized it was a romantic night."

Another night, Cruise and Kidman had dinner with a small group from the film, and began belting out tunes from *The Music Man* and *Oklahoma!* "The restaurant had a piano player," said one member of Cruise's inner circle. "That's all it took."

Family became part of the production. Tom brought Connor, dangling in a baby harness, around the set. "We were in the middle of this meeting," said production designer Norman Reynolds, "and Tom said, 'You haven't met my baby yet' and introduced us."

The kids spent more time with Cruise as Kidman began rehearsals for *Portrait of a Lady*.

Isabella spent half the days in school and the other half on the set. "Tom would say, 'I'm over here, honey,'" Jon Voight recalled. "You'd hear a 'Where, Daddy?' and then you'd hear a 'On top of the train, honey.'"

Cruise had to be physically involved in *Mission*, to the point of doing some of his own stunts. There were three biggies: hanging upside-down while downloading information from a CIA computer, getting whacked by a huge tidal wave that came spilling from a giant aquarium and, of course, the famous Chunnel train sequence, with the wind blowing in his face at 175 miles per hour.

De Palma said Cruise was not real happy about the water shoot. "We blow up a restaurant with all these aquariums in it," De Palma said. "And tons of water comes cascading around Tom. We had done it with the stunt guy, but we said, 'Tom, we have to do it with you or it's not convincing.' He walked over to me with the sweetest look on his face and said, 'Brian, I'm only an actor.' I said, 'Tom, just do it' and he did it. But I swear he could've drowned."

The train scene cost more to shoot — millions more — and there was wrangling over the scene. "Bob thought he could resolve the movie with a character revelation," De Palma said. "I'd constructed a high-speed chase scene on top of the train and I thought the movie needed this visceral ending to work. The cost was huge. Tom arbitrated and, at one point, I said, 'Let's try Bob's.' But in the end, Tom ultimately sided with me."

Cruise, however, was in control of the production — to the point of reworking the film's theme music. An orchestra in Los Angeles had spent three hours recording it — but Cruise sent it back and had it redone, saying he wanted to hear more flutes.

The plot of *Mission: Impossible* was incomprehensible and had so many twists and turns it was almost comical. No one, it seemed, followed the movie from beginning to end. But it didn't matter. The nonstop action, the stunts and, of course, the presence of Cruise, made it a blockbuster. *Mission* earned an amazing $75 million in its first six days in theaters.

"I'm not sure I could pass a test on the plot of *Mission: Impossible*," wrote one reviewer. "My consolation is the screenwriters probably couldn't, either ... But the bottom line on a film like this is: Tom Cruise looks cool and holds our attention while doing things that we don't quite understand — doing them so quickly and with so much style that we put our questions on hold and go with the flow."

Another reviewer wrote: "Having held the patent for more than a decade on Hollywood's notion of a yuppie conqueror with a gold-plated conscience, Tom Cruise has found the perfect superhero character on which to graft his breathlessly gung-ho screen personality."

The story, the writer added, "has enough twists and surprises to keep audiences guessing until the last minute. If that story doesn't make a shred of sense on any level, so what? Neither did the television series, in which basic credibility didn't matter so long as its sci-fi popular mechanics kept up the suspense." The film, the review summed up, was "the wildest movie ride of the year."

Chapter 18

HEROES

TOM CRUISE PLAYED THE HERO in almost every one of his 18 movies through *Mission: Impossible*. And, as that movie opened in 1996, Cruise got to play the hero in real life. He was driving through Santa Monica on March 4 of that year when he saw the crumpled, bloodied body of a woman laying on Wilshire Boulevard — and immediately pulled over.

Heloisa Vinhas lay in the road, having been

run down by a motorist as she crossed the busy, rain-soaked street. "I have no money," she said. "It's gonna be my birthday soon ... Don't let me die, don't let me die."

Others passing by had already called for emergency help, but Cruise stayed with the woman as she lay on the street, holding her hand and telling her to hang in there. He followed the ambulance to UCLA Medical Center — and when he learned she had no insurance, he volunteered to pay the stranger's medical bill, a whopping $7,000.

"It would have been easier for Tom just to keep going, especially since there were already people there," a pal said. "But Tom is a really good person and it just isn't in his nature to ignore another human being in distress."

Cruise paced the floor of the hospital until 4 a.m. the next day, when doctors assured him Vinhas was going to be all right.

Vinhas at the time didn't know Cruise had been her hero. "Tom is a very nice man, the best," she said later.

It was the type of random act of kindness that a publicist couldn't script — and Cruise's concern was genuine. After finding out later she was an aspiring actress — and what were the odds of that in Los Angeles? — he arranged for Vinhas to get a small part in his next film, *Jerry Maguire*.

At the London premiere of *Mission: Impossible*

it was Cruise to the rescue again. As he made his way through a corridor of fans, the crowd almost crushed two small boys against the police barricades. Cruise lifted both boys up from the surging crowd and handed them to police. "We are very grateful to Tom," said the mother of one boy.

But Cruise wasn't done. Several months later, Cruise and his family were on vacation, cruising on a yacht off the island of Capri in the Mediterranean. He spotted a fire on a sailboat and five people bobbing on a raft and immediately charged to their rescue — and brought all five aboard just as the stricken 63-foot vessel sank.

"If I ever get in trouble," said Tom's delighted publicist Pat Kingsley, "I hope Tom Cruise is nearby."

"It's not the greatest thing in the world to be rescued by me," said Cruise. "The next day, everyone comes knocking on the door."

When not out rescuing people, all was well at the Cruise-Kidman home. The couple talked publicly of their love for each other, Nicole even revealing they had "a song," Van Morrison's *Someone Like You.* The words: *I've been searching a long time for someone exactly like you. I've been traveling all around the world waiting for you to come through.*

"Like that song says," Nicole said, "I was looking for someone who could spend the rest of their life with me."

And life had become ... kids and work. "When we're in her bedroom, she's the teacher and we're the children," Kidman said of now 3-year-old Isabella. "She's bossing us around. She's, 'Now, darlings, sit down and I'll sing you a song.' Then she'll be the mommy. She'll order us to sleep on her bedroom floor and Tom ... well, Tom, he falls asleep."

Tom described a parenting technique he used for little Connor. "I say yes. He says no. I say no. He says yes. So anytime I want him to do something, I tell him he can't do it and he says yes and goes and does it. We're just trying to figure the damn thing out."

Cruise said all people needed to know about his marriage was that he and Nicole were deeply in love. "I go where she's going," he said. "Or she goes where I go. I think what's important is that kids see parents who love each other."

Pals said Cruise was the most henpecked husband in Hollywood — and added that he loved it. The sources claimed that Nicole, among other things, had made Cruise ditch his Los Angeles Dodger season tickets because she didn't want him off two or three nights a week, and also claimed Nicole treated him like "a servant," once making him drive miles from a movie location to buy fresh fruits and vegetables.

"But he loves her so much it never even

occurs to him that he's henpecked," said a pal. Whatever the facts about being "henpecked," it's true that he and Nicole kept their romance alive by spending as much time as possible together. Despite having small children, Tom and Nicole snuck out from time to time. "Sometimes we go out to dinner and stay up until about 2, 3 in the morning and wake up the kids," Cruise said. "They chat and play games, and then they go back to sleep. It's wild."

They lived in a big, comfortable house in the Pacific Palisades, which only a smattering of other stars called home. And they indulged themselves in a mountaintop vacation home in Vail, Colorado, and a smaller place in Sydney, Australia, where the family could stay when they visited Nicole's parents and family. Otherwise, "We're always working and on the road," said Cruise.

Cruise, however, occasionally played pickup hockey on Sunday nights, just like a regular fella. "I just ask them to stay away from my face," he said. "I say, 'Guys, I've got to be able to go in front of the cameras in the morning.'"

And the couple had arrived at a mutual support agreement: Whosoever turn it was to be working was allowed to be the movie star. "You are not allowed to be the one to freak out if you are not working," said Nicole. "If you are working, then you are allowed to be hysterical, anything, the whole roller-coaster of emotions."

But like any couple, they had their issues. "There are moments when we say this honeymoon is on pause for the next two hours while we get things worked out," he said. "You really only learn about yourself by that stuff that bounces back in your face."

It was Tom's turn to be the movie star again, Nicole having done *Portrait of a Lady* following the exhausting *Mission* production. Ironically, given all the heroic real-life acts mentioned above, Cruise, this time, was not playing the hero in 1996's *Jerry Maguire*. A character-driven drama, *Maguire* did away with special effects and impossible missions and told a fairly simple story of a high-powered sports agent who learns to stop and smell the roses.

The film put Cruise — who earned $20 million for the role — with director Cameron Crowe for the first time. Crowe, a former wunderkind reporter for *Rolling Stone*, made the switch to film and scored successes with the autobiographical *Fast Times at Ridgemont High* and *Say Anything*. Crowe paid homage to *Rolling Stone* founder Jann Wenner by casting him as the owner of the sports agency at which Jerry Maguire works in the film. Having Tom Cruise aboard for *Maguire* elevated Crowe to a new level as a director and was a huge payoff for the four years he had spent writing and researching the script for *Maguire*.

The movie paired Cruise with Renee Zellweger as the love interest and Cuba Gooding Jr. as the sole client Maguire has left after he has a meltdown in which he issues a "mission statement" that calls for his fellow agents to stop treating their athlete clients as cattle and start treating them as people.

But just calling for change — and Maguire gets fired for his epiphany — doesn't mean he is instantly transformed into a better human being. The film explores his journey from standard Cruise — callow and cool — to enlightened soul. And the film created a parallel to Cruise's own career arc, some felt, in the transformation of the hotshot, call-ya-later Maguire into a character who can really feel, just as Cruise's own life experience brought more depth and humanity to his choice of roles and his actual acting abilities.

As one reviewer put it, Maguire is "a mean, noncommittal Ken doll who has to work long and hard to be good, and who had to be good before he can be happy ... His soul is alive for the first time, but it's just an embryo. Crowe and Cruise cooperate beautifully in satirizing the image it took Cruise years to build."

"Your perception of this guy was winner, winner, winner and then to see him losing, fighting for acceptance," Crowe said. "And even in the most savage kind of revealing moments that he has to play, sometimes in front of hundreds of extras, it was a joyful thing for him."

Though Zellweger, playing single mom Dorothy Boyd, was a bit clingy and needy, the film was a success for Cruise. There were no vampires, no wigs, no exploding water tanks — just Cruise, naked and alone, traversing the route from insensitive heel to warm — but not fuzzy — lover and stepfather.

Cuba Gooding Jr., playing NFL receiver Rod Tidwell, got the signature line ("Show me the money!") and the Oscar for best supporting actor, but viewers came away with a new respect for the acting abilities of Cruise, who was nominated for an Oscar but lost again.

The other signature line from the film — "help me help you" — came from a frustrating moment during shooting. Gooding — who was just "f***ing with Tom," according to director Crowe — decided to give Tom no help during a scene. "Tom just got so frustrated," Crowe said, "he started going, 'Help me help you, help me help you.' "

"In *Jerry Maguire*, Cruise plays the same old smoothie," wrote one reviewer. "This time, he's a sports agent. But a witty script and Cameron Crowe's sensitive direction expose the hysteria, the downright sickness, beneath Cruise's standard persona. Cruise plays along, laying himself out for laughs, and the result is a surprisingly fresh didactic comedy that preaches the hollowness of glamour and status and the American cult of winning."

His co-stars raved as well. "His acting was so good it was almost bizarre," Zellweger said later. "You'd look into his eyes and he'd really be there, he'd really be in love with you. You could see his heart and soul ... and then the director would yell 'Cut,' Tom would leave the set and you'd have to go into therapy for six months."

Chapter 19

SEX

CRUISE ONCE AGAIN PROVED his bankability with *Maguire*. The film earned an amazing $154 million — the fifth Cruise film in a row to earn more than $100 million. He hadn't had a clunker, in fact, since the dismal *Far and Away*, in which he starred with Nicole. Now, with Nicole by his side once again, Cruise decided to test his appeal and his audience's loyalty in a film that would place him way out of character and pair him with yet another legendary director.

The director was Stanley Kubrick, auteur of such hugely influential films as *2001: A Space Odyssey, Lolita, A Clockwork Orange* and *Full Metal Jacket.* The reclusive Kubrick, an expatriate American living and working in London, didn't make many films and the release of each of his movies was an event. Putting Cruise with such a master seemed on face an anomaly and created a buzz similar to that which had greeted Cruise's casting as the vampire Lestat. But Kubrick had sought out Cruise — and Kidman — for his new film *Eyes Wide Shut* and that fact alone tempered much of the wonderment at the leap Cruise was about to take.

The film explored a married couple's sexuality and would entail a 19-month stint in London. The film was to be grueling and would ultimately force Tom and Nicole to go spelunking into caverns in their own relationship that they felt might better be left alone. But Cruise, the $70 million man, was ready to step off a cliff — again.

"I don't feel I've done everything that I wanna do," he explained. "I feel good about stuff I've done and I've learned — good and bad — but I don't feel like I've done it yet. I don't feel like I'm ... finished. In acting, as good as you are today, it's a different experience every time you go out, every movie. It's not like basketball, where as you get older your skills are there but maybe your speed is gone.

"People keep telling you, 'Wait until you get into your 30s, the roles keep getting better and deeper,'" he added. "And you realize, maybe I'll have more to offer in life experience. But then you get there and there's no rulebook. There's no rulebook as to what a great movie is or what a perfect moment is. It changes and you have to keep evolving. You've got to keep working — and that's what's fun. That's the challenge of it."

Kubrick faxed an offer to star in his next film to Cruise — and Cruise, eager to work with Kubrick, traveled to England for a reading at Kubrick's estate outside London.

Eyes Wide Shut was based upon a 1926 novella by Arthur Schnitzler, which told the story of Fridolin and his wife, Albertina. Set over the course of two nights, the couple investigate more and more dangerous sexual fantasies — Fridolin at one point fantasizing that he is seducing a dead patient's daughter, while Albertina dreamed of her husband being crucified at an orgy. "It's difficult to find any writer who understood the human soul more truly and who had a more profound insight into the way people think, act and really are," Kubrick said of Schnitzler.

Kubrick and Frederic Raphael wrote the screenplay for *Eyes*, updating it, so the rumors said, setting it in New York. Cruise was to play a medical doctor and Kidman a curator.

Tom, Nicole and their children headed to England in November 1996 and were secreted away on a guarded set outside London during the production. They knew they were in for a torturous and long shoot and became semi-residents, buying a $1.4 million penthouse suite in a mansion for themselves.

"We were going to do what it took to do this picture, whatever time, because I felt — and Nic did, too — that this was going to be a really special time for us," Cruise said. "We knew it would be difficult. But I would have absolutely kicked myself if I hadn't done this."

Cruise and Kidman essentially disappeared for a year. Secrecy enveloped the project. One article was headlined: Where in the World Is Tom Cruise? — and there was much speculation about the film, with one publication saying the couple "intensely researched the real-life world of sex and drugs for their steamy roles."

But as filming went on and on — 15 months by one count — the Cruises adapted to a normal life in jolly old England. Among other humdrum activities, Sydney Pollack, who had directed Cruise in *The Firm* but appeared as an actor in *Eyes Wide Shut,* revealed that he taught Cruise how to barbecue ribs on-set.

"I started him off with simple recipes such as spareribs," Pollack said. "He'd watch me and write it all down. Sometimes he'd videotape it. He's a very thorough and serious guy. He's a great cook now."

"We really enjoy life in England," Cruise said, noting that he'd spent time there shooting *Mission: Impossible* prior to *Eyes.* "We are able to live normal lives there. We take the kids to the movies. We go shopping. We go to the park."

There were reports that Kubrick was demanding, making the actors do take after take. Much time was burned with just the three of them — Kubrick and his famous charges — sitting in a room, talking about sexual obsession. Kidman claimed not to mind the slow but intense pace. "I don't find it grueling," Kidman said early in the production. "Other directors say, 'OK, two takes, let's move on, come on, we've got to go, we're losing time.' Kubrick doesn't care about the schedule or anything."

And Cruise had his own reputation for perfection by this point. "He's incredibly persistent and focused, and he'll drive you completely insane because he keeps coming at it and at it and at it," said David Koepp, the screenwriter on *Mission: Impossible*. Still, Cruise was said to have developed a stomach ulcer during the filming.

Kubrick came to be something of a surrogate father as the filming dragged on. "They spent a lot of mornings together, and Stanley spent a lot of time with their kids," said Kubrick friend Julian Senior.

"He was like a father," Kidman said. "He understood your humanity and reveled in your dedication."

When time came to film Cruise and Kidman in the nude scene that opened the film, Kubrick closed the set and operated the camera himself, only intensifying the trio's relationship.

"It was a dream come true to work with Stanley Kubrick," Cruise said. "I learned a lot about filmmaking from him. It's true that he would fax me changes in the script in the middle of the night and that it wasn't unusual for him to do 20 takes of a scene, but sometimes we did a scene in one take. He was intense but also inspiring and funny."

"For me it was no sacrifice," Cruise added. "He became a dear friend and a mentor. Sometimes I'd look at him and think, 'This guy made *2001*!' I'll carry the experience the rest of my life."

Kubrick was happy to take his famous co-stars under his wing. "He becomes very close and

involved with the lives of his lead actors," said a
friend.

Filming was thought to be done in January
1998. Cruise and Kidman and their children
headed back to the United States and headed to
the state of Washington, where Nicole was set
to star opposite Sandra Bullock in *Practical
Magic*. But in their absence, Kubrick suddenly
added another character, played by Thomas
Gibson, and Cruise was called back to England
to re-shoot some scenes.

Cruise went on to pre-production work on
Mission: Impossible 2 and to prepare for a role
in a Paul Thomas Anderson film while Kubrick
put *Eyes Wide Shut* together. The secrecy about
the film remained, except for one titillating 90-
second snippet that leaked out. The snippet was
"one of the most mesmerizingly erotic scenes
ever committed to film," according to one writer
who viewed it.

No one else was allowed to see it. When the
movie was screened for Tom and Nicole in New
York, the projectionist was ordered to let it roll
and then step outside the booth.

The film, so long in the making, was finally
set for a July 1999 release. But devastating news
reached Tom and Nicole on March 7 of that
year. Kubrick, who had finished and submitted
Eyes Wide Shut to the studio only four days

previously, died of a heart attack. Leon Vitali, Kubrick's longtime assistant, broke the news to Cruise in a 3 a.m. phone call.

"Devastation and horror don't describe his reaction," said Vitali. "This was the most established relationship I've seen in 30 years between Stanley and one of his stars. And the deeper they got into filming, the more relaxed and open it became."

Cruise described a "moment of real loss and pain that I hadn't felt for a while. I mean shock — absolute shock. And Nic had never had anyone pass away that she had been that close to, ever. That was a very difficult time. But you've got to bounce back, because you've got your children. Here's this dear friend that you've lost — and immediately life is making you put it into perspective. Whereas when you're a child, if your parents divorced, that's your whole world."

Cruise and Kidman flew to London for Kubrick's funeral on March 12. They retained high hopes for the film, even as they grieved for the demanding director. And Cruise had no regrets over the time spent on the film, time which according to one estimate cost Cruise between $40 million and $80 million in terms of projects lost.

But Cruise claimed not to care. "I don't want to sit down when I'm 70 and say I've wasted my time away and not made the films I wanted to make," he said.

When the film was released July 16, it became apparent that many of the rumors about the film had been dead wrong. The most widely reported rumor — that the film was about two married therapists who cheat on each other with their patients — also was mistaken.

They were a couple — Dr. Bill and Alice Harford, rich Manhattanites. After teasing each other at a lavish Christmas party, Alice (Kidman) confesses while they're both high on marijuana her lust for and readiness to cheat on the doctor with a young Naval officer she encountered the summer before. After a long fight in the bedroom, the doctor leaves and wanders the streets of New York, an odyssey into a "wild, shadowlike succession of gloomy and lascivious adventures, all without an end," in the words of the novella. Dr. Harford's odyssey leads him to a masked orgy — the filming of which was altered after Kubrick's death as people were digitally altered to cover enough flesh for the film to keep its R rating.

Eyes Wide Shut was "a brilliantly provocative *tour de force*," wrote one reviewer. "Its powerful and lingering resonance attest to a final compassion and profundity in Kubrick, the body-and-soul commitment of Cruise and Ms. Kidman, and the Rorschach-like ability of this material to envelop audiences in ways unexplained and unexpected."

Was there nudity? Yes, with Kidman slipping out of her dress in the film's first sequence, the orgy scene and other revealing shots. "*Eyes Wide Shut* is an adult film in every atom of its being," wrote Roger Ebert. "For adult audiences, it creates a mesmerizing daydream of sexual fantasy."

The critics couldn't save the film from the negative press it had received during its long gestation, however. It had "bad buzz," as its esoteric form and plot seemed to go straight over some viewers' heads and left them to advise others to skip it. Even the prospect of seeing Tom and Nicole argue in their underwear couldn't bring audiences in and the film ended Cruise's string of $100-million-plus films, earning just above $55 million.

It was most definitely not a Tom Cruise Picture — but that didn't mean he was done with that genre. Despite the financial failing of the movie — it barely broke even — Cruise could still do whatever he wanted.

"You never really know what's going to be a hit," Cruise said. "I've already made a lot of money. Money isn't the reason I make movies. I just hope that the studios make back the money they spend on the movies they let me make, so that I can make pictures for a little longer. That's all I ask for; the chance to make more movies."

Chapter 20

BEING FRANK

THE GRUELING SHOOT ON *Eyes Wide
Shut* forced Nicole and Tom to examine
intimate issues in their marriage.

"Working together in *Eyes Wide Shut* made us
deal with things and talk about things that we
normally wouldn't talk about," Nicole said.
"Because they are too dangerous. The territory
was too dangerous. It was all about obsession
and jealousy and all those emotions you're usually

trying to quell. We were opening doors that can be very dangerous. We came out of it a lot closer. We became so attuned to each other and are still discovering things about each other."

But there were issues. Among them were where to put down roots. Kidman intimated that she was tiring of Los Angeles "because it's so much about movie talk. It's money, money, money." Sydney was under consideration, as were New York and London. "Probably London is best because it's so low-key and different," Kidman said. "They don't hound our children there. The London press is more respectful."

Still, despite the financial failure that followed the intense work on *Eyes*, to friends all seemed well in the very private recesses of the Cruise-Kidman household. And Cruise would soon show the world that he was at the top of his game professionally, as well.

With *Eyes* done, Cruise forged ahead with the sequel to *Mission: Impossible*. The film was a sure moneymaker — after all, the first film had been a blockbuster hit — but just to ensure that it was done right, Cruise brought in director John Woo, who had an affinity for special effects and plot twists and turns. Cruise also brought in his favorite script doctor, Robert Towne. Starting pretty much from scratch again, Towne wrote *M:I-2* around action scenes that Woo had already envisioned and mapped out for the movie. It was not exactly going to be a talky drama.

While work proceeded on *M:I-2*, Cruise indulged himself in a different kind of project — an ensemble drama. The film was *Magnolia*, written by Paul Thomas Anderson, an up-and-coming auteur who received raves for *Boogie Nights*, a funny-sad look at the California porn industry in the 1970s.

Anderson and Cruise had hooked up while he and Nicole were in England still working on *Eyes Wide Shut*. Cruise invited Anderson to visit the set and Anderson wound up with a tour of the place given by none other than his hero Stanley Kubrick. Several months later, Anderson called Cruise and said, 'Listen, I've written this role for you, would you be interested in doing it?' " Cruise recalled.

"I knew I was going to make it right from the beginning," Cruise said of *Magnolia*. "But we had to work out the dates, because Nic and I have been together 10 years and we've never been separated more than two weeks."

Magnolia told the story of 11 characters whose lives intersected — randomly or not — over the course of a day in the San Fernando Valley. Cruise played Frank T.J. Mackey, a sleazy, misogynist motivational guru who catered to women-hating men. We first see Cruise leading one of his misguided "Seduce and Destroy" seminars, urging his male viewers who have been spurned, dumped and ignored to turn the tables.

Cruise characterized his role as "just a gift from Paul Thomas Anderson. I've read a lot of different scripts and thought: 'Well, I'd like to see this,' but ... With *Magnolia* I thought: 'This could be wild. I mean, I could really fail here! I could really f**k this up, make a total ass out of myself. This could be a real pie in the face, you know? I've gotta do it!' "

Though the actual filming of Cruise's part would take only 10 days, he leaped into the role of Frank T.J. Mackey. "We were working on what my character was going to look like, so I started letting my hair grow," Cruise said. "The first wardrobe thing was golf pants and golf shirts, and I said, 'I always saw him wearing an armband.' Because I picked up clues out of the script — it says he's a superhero; he thinks of himself as one of these superhero guys — and I was thinking of *The Rainmaker* and *All That Jazz*: those leather-wrist, masculine hero kind of things. There was a certain point where I was just on it with the character. And Paul trusted that."

Cruise gave a ferocious turn as the pumped-up, scary, but charismatic Mackey. "I had so much fun playing those scenes," he said. "I had some friends, you know, 'come on down and see this,' and I got so much enjoyment out of seeing Paul just pissing himself on the takes."

There was more than just bombast to the role, however — much more. Toward the end of the film, Mackey must attend to his dying, estranged father, played by Jason Robards. The confrontation between father and son was exhausting, yet exhilarating.

"You just lose yourself," Cruise said. "I was exhausted. Jason Robards ... I think he was a little exhausted, because he's got to be there, and the first thing he heard was, 'You c***sucker ... you f***ing c***sucker.' It's a very fine balance when you're doing those scenes, because you're out there on the edge, and there are things you can't necessarily be responsible for when you go to those places."

Cruise wound up being nominated for an Oscar. "In a blazing performance, Cruise is a revelation," said one reviewer. "Cruise seethes with the chaotic energy of a wounded animal — he's devastating." The film itself, the reviewer said, "is a near miracle."

Another writer said of *Magnolia*: "Its single biggest surprise is Tom Cruise in the role of a strutting, obscenity-spouting cult figure named Frank Mackey."

Though Cruise's strong performance seemed

to take many by surprise, he never doubted his ability — and also gave some credit to the character himself. "Everyone is just kind of going, 'Jeeeez,' " he said. "I remember someone said, 'How come you haven't played a character like this before?' I said, 'Please tell me in the last 15 years where this character has been.' "

M:I-2 brought Cruise down to earth — and Tom Cruise back to his core audience. Filmed in Utah and Australia — where Tom and his family settled for a year as he worked on *M:I-2* and Nicole began work on *Moulin Rouge* — the film wasn't going to get Cruise an Oscar nomination, but it was certainly going to get him money. Lots of money. Once again, Cruise took no up-front money to produce and star in the film, and even covered the beyond-budget costs of making it — and still walked away with a cool $75 million when all was said and done.

M:I-2 was a film made for fun as well as money, however. It brought Cruise back as Ethan Hunt and this time the movie version of the TV show paid homage to various film influences, including Alfred Hitchcock.

"Tom loved the cleverness of this group of people from the Impossible Missions Force who would solve problems by abandoning traditional methodology," said his longtime agent Paula Wagner. "The series was very intelligent, and it had all the elements loved by audiences: romance and drama, with adventure and action built in." Actually, it was the other way around, considering how the plot was being contrived around action sequences.

But, noted Wagner, "*M:I-2* is different from the first film as it focuses on a more personal story. We get to see a more romantic side to Ethan Hunt within the framework of an exciting action drama."

It was camp — but in a good way. And it was fun from the start. "Cruise's Ethan Hunt receives his mission from a pair of sunglasses on top of a mountain in Utah," a writer noted of the plot. "He throws them away and they self-destruct. The title appears and then it self-destructs."

The plot had Cruise and his female comrade, played by Thandie Newton, racing around the world trying to prevent bad-guy Sean Ambrose (Dougray Scott) from unleashing a manufactured virus on the world. It was an action thriller — but there was time for send-ups, too: Tom's famous smile, comic-book dialogue, a plot vaguely reminiscent of Hitchcock's *Notorious*. One writer noted that while *M:I-2* was "hardly a model of transparency," it was "Dick and Jane next to its grimly unfathomable 1996 predecessor. The sequel ... has a freer sense of humor and more swank exoticism. It does Hitchcock, it does Bond and it has a pert little number named Thandie Newton."

M:I-2 was what it was. Cruise gave his audience what they wanted, what they'd come to expect from him, and they responded in kind. *M:I-2* swamped even its older brother at the box office, raking in almost $213 million.

Tom took a deep breath after completing *M:I-2*. It was Nicole's turn to be the movie star. They'd both worked furiously during their year in Australia — he on *M:I-2* and Nicole on the musical *Moulin Rouge*. They were now set to move to Madrid for a supernatural thriller, *The Others*, in which Kidman would star and Cruise would produce. But before leaving Australia, and while Nicole finished work on *Moulin*, Cruise took off for a vacation with Isabella and Connor, setting sail in the waters off Australia. It was supposed to be relaxing.

It turned into a nightmare. "We're like the Griswolds," Cruise confessed, referring to the *National Lampoon's Summer Vacation* couple. Piloting a 40-foot converted fishing boat named *Alibi*, Cruise fretted as the motor conked out, a jet skier slammed into the side of the boat, the good ship ground onto a reef — and, adding insult to injury, a fiery inferno erupted as Cruise was cooking, forcing him to tip the cooking contraption into the water to save the boat.

Cruise, a wag noted, became "the first actor in Aussie history to throw a barbie on the shrimp" with that act. Cruise dutifully put on his scuba gear and went after the barbecue, however. "It was tragic," Isabella said later. "Then fun."

Chapter 21

SPLIT

I T WAS DEC. 28, 2000 — just three days from New Year's Eve. Cruise and Kidman were spending some of the holidays in Las Vegas and at 12:30 a.m., they decided to pull rank at the Stratosphere Casino Hotel and Tower. Cruise called security and asked for a ride on Big Shot, a thrill ride atop the hotel's 1,149-foot tower. Officials acceded to the very famous couple's wish, closing the roof deck to mere mortals so Tom and Nicole could get their early-morning kicks. They strapped into the 12-seat car and were soon hurtling 160 feet into the air. "Tom Cruise just had a huge grin on his face," a ride supervisor said. "They rode it about three times. They kept screaming, 'One more time!' They had a blast."

"We are so close," Kidman said in 1999, "that we finish each other's sentences and read each other's minds. I found somebody that I want to spend the rest of my life with. We are committed and I can't picture my life without him."

On Dec. 24 — their 10th anniversary — Tom and Nicole renewed their wedding vows before a small group of friends and family at their Los Angeles home. They seemed as much in love as ever. In fact, the lives of Cruise and Kidman seemed to be a continuing fairy tale. She was the princess, he the knight in shining armor. They hopscotched the globe with their kids, earning millions of dollars plus the adulation of fans.

Then, seemingly overnight, everything changed.

From out of the blue — at least to their fans, the media and even close friends — Tom Cruise's publicist Pat Kingsley announced Feb. 5 the couple was separating.

"Citing the difficulties inherent in their divergent careers which constantly kept them apart, they concluded that an amicable separation seemed best for both of them at this time." Just two days later, as the world was still digesting the news of the split, Cruise filed for divorce.

Nothing seemed to make sense in that simple sentence. Hadn't Cruise said over and over that he and Nicole had never spent more than 12 days apart? Hadn't they reveled in their family, in finding in each other their soul mate, in supporting each other through thick and thin? How their marriage had grown stronger through the grueling introspection of *Eyes Wide Shut*?

Nicole was said to have been as blindsided as anyone by Tom's announcement and all indications were that he was pulling the strings. One of Nicole's friends allowed, however, that trouble between the two had been developing for some time. "Nicole was surprised by the timing of the announcement more than the idea of the separation," her friend said. "It came much sooner than expected."

"Nicole was shattered by the brutal suddenness with which Tom filed for divorce," said another pal. "At first it was agreed that they'd separate, discuss their situation in six months and see whether there was a prospect of reconciliation. Then without any warning he filed for divorce."

Looking back, clues indeed appeared that things weren't right between Cruise and

Kidman, despite the renewal of their wedding vows just weeks before the split. Nicole was seen in public Feb. 2 dressed as if in mourning. She looked upset as she lunched with her agent, witnesses said. And Jan. 21, Tom and Nicole hardly interacted at the Golden Globe awards.

"Tom and Nicole arrived separately and during the festivities avoided each other like the plague," a source said. Nicole seemed to flirt openly with awards presenter George Clooney.

Another friend claimed that the couple split a week before the announcement. "It was obvious by the last week of January that the marriage was over. Tom moved out of the house. He was filming his latest movie, *Vanilla Sky*, at the Paramount studio and staying somewhere nearby. Nicole was alone at the house with their two adopted kids. The only visitors were lawyers."

And what was this "trouble" between Cruise and Kidman? Reported theories ran rampant: That she wanted to relocate to Sydney and he didn't. That she was jealous of his career. That she was an "ice queen" who used Cruise to further her own career.

Tom now was reported to have been jealous of a variety of males with whom Kidman had been associated. There was Iain Glenn, Nicole's co-star in *The Blue Room*. There was fellow

Aussie star Russell Crowe, a mutually admitted good friend, who was said to have inspired a tantrum in Cruise when he publicly held hands with Nicole. There was Ewan McGregor, Nicole's co-star in *Moulin Rouge*.

While the public — and, supposedly, Nicole herself — wondered why Cruise moved so abruptly to end the marriage, Cruise himself stayed cryptic.

"She knows why," Cruise said. "And I know why. She's the mother of my children and I wish her well. And I think you just move on. And I don't say that lightly. I don't say that with anything. Things happen in life and you do everything you can, and in every possible way, and there's a point at which you just sometimes have to face the brutal reality."

And later, Cruise was adamant in saying he didn't care about the curiosity over the divorce.

"So? You've got lingering questions," he told one writer. "OK. And? I really don't give a s**t. Get a f***ing life. Talk about something that's a little more important."

Cruise's take on his divorce from Nicole echoed his take on his first divorce from Mimi Rogers. "My divorce was just something that needed to be done," he had said of his split from Mimi.

In both instances, Tom moved into full Cruise

Control. Within seven days of Cruise's filing for divorce from Nicole, "she was in a room with Tom and a bunch of agents haggling over their business matters," a source said. Nicole's head was still spinning, by all accounts, as Cruise coldly made his move. "She could not contain herself and right in front of everyone asked, 'Why, Tom? After 10 years of marriage, why are you doing this?,' " added the source. "Nicole honestly doesn't know what happened."

The public relations war fought out in the media seemed to favor Nicole as the victim. But Cruise's friend Sydney Pollack — who spent months with the couple while doing *The Firm* and *Eyes Wide Shut* — said Cruise, who had moved out of the couple's Pacific Palisades home and into a posh Beverly Hills hotel, was hurting, too.

"I don't think for a moment he's not feeling pain about the split — I know he is," Pollack said. "He is not going around complaining to magazines and talking to people about it. Tom is a very disciplined guy. He's getting on with his life — being a professional and being the best father he can be under the circumstances."

There was much at stake beyond the emotional aspects of the split. Tom's fortune was estimated to be $325 million — and a legal fine point arose, which Nicole, even as she struggled to understand Tom's motives, had to address. Under California law, a couple married for 10 years or more were each entitled to an exact 50-50 split of assets upon divorce. Cruise claimed in legal papers that the split had occurred in December, prior to their 10th anniversary. Nicole claimed they had been intimate until Feb. 4, the day before the announcement of separation.

And there was another bombshell to complicate matters and feed a hungry press: On March 16, Nicole Kidman miscarried. The fetus was said to have been 13 weeks old, indicating that Tom and Nicole had been intimate, indeed, around the time of their 10th anniversary.

But was it Tom's baby? Friends said Nicole desperately hoped her pregnancy, once revealed, would cause Cruise to reconcile with her — a hope which was dashed when she miscarried. "Nicole was hoping the tragedy would help melt Tom's heart and win him back," a pal said. "But he said that they were finished for good."

Nicole's tragedy began fueling speculation that the pregnancy was the smoking gun in his seemingly sudden decision to divorce Nicole.

"She knows why." It's all anyone ever got from Tom, at least on the record, and Tom moved quickly to settle with Nicole and keep details of their marriage out of the public eye. Cruise was said to have assumed total control of the divorce and wanted things to go smoothly.

"He told his legal advisers to get the divorce done as quickly as possible," a pal said. "Tom has steamrolled Nicole — by allowing his lawyers to use every fast-track trick in the book to make her go away as quickly as possible." Cruise sought joint custody of Connor and Isabella and was said to be seeking a better than 50-50 split of the couple's assets. Cruise also asked for a bifurcated divorce, a process that would speed the resolution of the divorce.

Nicole, said one pal, "has been through what amounts to a legal mugging. Simply put, Tom wields a tremendous amount of power in Hollywood. He can get anything that he wants."

"Nicole feels that she's lost any influence she may have had in the film industry as the wife of America's No.1 box-office star," the friend revealed. "She literally may be blackballed if she doesn't cave in to Tom's demands."

"All I can say is, it's been awful," Kidman told Oprah Winfrey. "One of those things where you just say, 'I cannot believe this is happening to me.'"

It was an amazingly bitter end to Hollywood's favorite love story.

Chapter 22

SKY

CRUISE WAS EMBARKING ON a new love story — one which had almost eerie resemblances to his relationship with the now deposed Ms. Kidman.

His new love was Penelope Cruz, a beautiful, raven-haired Spanish actress who perhaps not so coincidentally happened to be his co-star in his next film, *Vanilla Sky*.

As with Kidman, whom Tom met during

pre-production for *Days of Thunder* almost 12 years before while he was still married to Mimi Rogers, Tom went out of his way to claim that he and Penelope had begun their romance only after he had filed for divorce. But that didn't stop speculation that Ms. Cruz had, in fact, been yet another reason that Tom had so coldly and abruptly filed for divorce from Nicole.

"He often kisses Penelope and gives her little hugs of affection," one insider on the set of *Vanilla Sky* noted before the couple's official "coming out." But when Tom and Penelope made it official on an exotic island vacation together in July 2001, friends claimed Nicole had suspected there was something between Tom and Penelope for a long time.

"Penelope is the one woman who's always gotten under Nicole's skin," a pal said. "In the early days of her breakup with Tom, Nicole kept saying that she didn't know why Tom ended the marriage so swiftly and suddenly. But in her heart, Nicole believes Penelope is one big reason her marriage crumbled."

The pal said Cruise had been intrigued with Cruz since he saw her in the movie *Abre los Ojos* in 1997. Cruise loved the movie so much, the pal said, he decided he wanted to remake it in English, and nab Cruz as his co-star. It was to be called *Vanilla Sky*.

Cruise teamed with his *Jerry Maguire* director Cameron Crowe on the flick and indeed landed Penelope as his leading lady. Cruz was no ingénue. She was a star in Spain and was now making forays into Hollywood. She had been linked to other co-stars — including Matt Damon in *All the Pretty Horses* and Nicolas Cage in *Captain Corelli's Mandolin*.

The timing of the incorporation of Cruise & Cruz intrigued Nicole — and friends said she may have thought that Tom plotted his divorce for more than a year as he became more and more beguiled by his co-star.

"I think Nicole believes that Tom was secretly in love with Penelope for months and months, while all the time telling Nicole they were 'just friends.' And she's angry!" a friend said. "She probably believes he plotted his getaway almost from the moment he met Penelope during pre-production meetings for *Vanilla Sky* and fell head over heels for her."

Nicole, for her part, raised eyebrows by vacationing with Russell Crowe and friends on the island of Fiji. Tom and Nicole booked time at a resort there the year before and decided to split the time there. The timing was almost comical: Nicole, Crowe and their friends and family left the island almost as Tom and Penelope, plus his sister Lee Anne and some friends, were flying in.

"Word quickly shot around the world that he was there with Penelope," a friend of Nicole's said. "When Nicole heard he was sharing the island with Penelope, she found she'd probably been dumped for another woman!"

It wasn't that simple, according to a friend of Tom's. "Tom tried to stop himself from falling for Penelope — but he couldn't," the friend said. "He felt something was missing from his marriage to Nicole. The passion had left the marriage and being with Penelope almost every day while filming *Vanilla Sky* rekindled flames he thought had died. He started preparing himself emotionally for the day when he would leave Nicole."

Cruise maintained he and Cruz became an item after *Vanilla Sky*.

"You know, I don't know the exact day," Cruise said of falling for Cruz. "It just kind of crept up. There was so much other stuff going on in my life. It doesn't happen quite like that, but, you see, she's a wonderful person, someone that I've had respect for. I worked with her and you see she's genuine and talented. She went off and made another picture. And, you know, we'd talk on the phone and, you know, it just evolved from there. With everything that was going on for me, that wasn't something I was looking for, quite honestly. But I'm very happy to have it."

Whatever the timing of the romance, Kidman

was not happy about Penelope. "She said, 'He flat- out swore to me up and down that there was nothing going on,'" a friend of Nicole's said. "She said, 'He obviously had her waiting in the wings and just waited until he started looking like a nice guy again.' All this time she's been wondering why the marriage ended and this could be it."

Not that it mattered. Cruise was demonstrating his ability to move on and not look back. But the past still continued to catch up with him.

Tom's girl trouble should have put to rest once and for all the ridiculously false rumors that he was gay. But in the midst of his divorce from Nicole and his blossoming romance with Penelope, the erroneous "gay issue" reared its ugly head again — and Cruise responded with a fury that demonstrated once again just who was going to control his image.

A porn star known as Chad Slater claimed in a French magazine that he had an affair with Cruise. Cruise fired off a $100 million lawsuit against Slater — also known as Kyle Bradford but whose real name was Phil Notaro. The suit claimed Slater's story was false and defamatory. The public, "believing that he had a homosexual affair ... will be less inclined to patronize Cruise's films, particularly since he tends to play parts calling for heterosexual romance and action adventure," Cruise's suit said.

Slater quickly caved and in an affidavit denied that he'd told the magazine or anyone else about any affair with Cruise. Cruise's attorney Bert Fields said Slater's story "is absolutely false. The man himself has denied it."

But wait — there's more. When a magazine publisher around the same time called media outlets and made cryptic, incorrect claims about the existence of a homosexual videotape of Cruise and another man, Cruise delivered another crushing $100 million lawsuit to the courts.

The publisher quickly learned a lesson in Cruise Control. But he steadfastly maintained that he did not have any such tape of Cruise and didn't even know if one existed. "Our twist on the Tom Cruise story was to offer a $500,000 reward to anyone who had proof, meaning a photo or videotape, that he is gay," *Bold* publisher Mike Davis said. "We were basically sending out a message — either put up or shut up. Then *Bold* magazine received an e-mail from a gentleman stating that he witnessed and participated in homosexual acts with Cruise and others and had a videotape of them having sex."

Davis began calling media outlets. "I never said there was definitely a tape," he said.

"Suddenly, Bert Fields is suing me and claiming to the media that I have a tape, that it's for sale and it's of Cruise having homosexual sex with ME! That's totally false."

The suits were a calculated risk on Cruise's part, according to prominent attorney Raoul Felder. He said if Cruise pursued the cases into court, he might be subject to exposure of his own sexual history.

"They can ask Cruise most anything," he said. "His past sexual history would become an open book."

If the lawsuits seemed an overreaction to some, to Cruise they achieved his goal — to protect his image, and to protect his children, from damaging lies. As Felder noted: "Those aren't lawsuits — those are terror weapons."

In the midst of the divorce, the lawsuits and the new romance, Cruise still had to show up for work. *Vanilla Sky* still had a month of shooting left when Cruise dropped his bombshell about the divorce and he might have been forgiven had he been a little distracted. But Cruise stayed focused, even gathering everyone on the set the day before the separation announcement to let them know he was still with them.

"It was right before a really intense scene in a club," one crew member said, "and he gathered everybody together and said, 'You're gonna hear something, it's gonna be on the radio and everywhere, and I'm going through a separation.' " But Cruise only rededicated himself to the movie. "It's all of us together," Cruise told them. "But I wanted you to know first."

The crew member added: "It meant a lot to people and made them acknowledge that it is a family making a movie and everybody worked a little harder and probably felt a little protective of him."

Although Cruise's psyche was in turmoil, he never showed it on the *Vanilla Sky* set. "Whatever personal pain he might have been going through, he never showed it on the set," said director Crowe.

Vanilla Sky told the increasingly complex story of self-obsessed David Aames, a magazine publisher who's happy to drift in and out of casual relationships until he meets Sofia, played by Cruz. Julie (Cameron Diaz), his latest conquest prior to meeting Sofia, learns of his attraction to Sofia and turns up the screws on Aames — forcing a car accident in which she is killed and Aames is grossly disfigured. Aames wakes from a coma, is provided with a latex mask by stumped doctors and begins a race against time to prove that he didn't kill Julie.

"As it leaves behind the real world and begins

exploring life as a waking dream ... *Vanilla Sky* loosens its emotional grip and becomes a disorganized and abstract if still-intriguing meditation on parallel themes," one reviewer said. "One is the quest for eternal life and eternal youth; another is guilt and the ungovernable power of the unconscious mind to undermine science's utopian discoveries.

"What carries the film is Mr. Cruise's impeccable marathon-man star turn in a performance that is characteristically icy beneath a bluff, glittering, ever-boyish charm."

Another reviewer noted that the choice of *Vanilla Sky* was an "intelligent and risky" one for Cruise, but summed up that for the actor, "the easy parts are too easy, the difficult parts are beyond his grasp."

Vanilla Sky was another ambitious leap for Cruise. Despite the obvious interest in the now very public romance with Penelope Cruz, however, the film had a slow start in theaters. Hoping to jump-start its box office receipts, Cruise and director Crowe embarked on a publicity tour that eventually wound itself around the world. Cruise and Crowe even called a Los Angeles reviewer who dissed the film and discussed the film for 90 minutes with him. "Every day was like another opportunity to show people who he really is, how much he loved the movie and how much he loves being alive," said Crowe. The efforts paid off: *Vanilla Sky*, which had started with a $20 million weekend and then gone immediately south, eventually raked in more than $100 million.

Chapter 23

GODFATHER

THERE WAS PLENTY OF unfinished business between Tom Cruise and Nicole Kidman. In an uncomfortable twist for both of them, there was still work to do on *The Others*, which starred Kidman and which Cruise was producing. And, of course, there was the divorce.

Cruise, as his pal Sydney Pollack had noted, wasn't talking about the divorce. He plunged into his next project — a film called *Minority Report* — the day after shooting was finished on *Vanilla Sky*. "I finished *Vanilla Sky*, shaved my head and began work on *Minority Report* the next day," he said.

But at least Cruise had an unexpected ally. Wife No. 1 — Mimi Rogers — came back into his life just as Tom was letting go of Wife No. 2 and gave Cruise the honor of becoming god-father to her baby boy Charlie.

Rogers married producer Chris Ciaffa and Charlie was her second child by him. Tom and Mimi had slowly developed a relationship in the intervening years since their divorce.

Cruise escorted Mimi to an AIDS benefit while in the early throes of his split from Kidman. "Tom was really down in the dumps at the time," a source said. "He turned to Mimi in his time of need." Mimi, seven months pregnant with Charlie, "asked him what he'd think about being the child's godfather — and Tom was genuinely touched."

At least Cruise had some closure in his life. That wasn't the case with Nicole, who assumed the role of victim very well and made small public swipes at Cruise. Her remarks were taken as perfectly allowable considering how she'd been so coldly dumped, at least as the matter was viewed by the public. Noting their discrepancy in height, Nicole joked that if nothing else, she could go back to wearing high heels. The comment was duly noted by the world's press, which was eager to see how Ms. Kidman would bounce back.

In April, several months after the divorce filing, Kidman had a coming out of sorts. She attended a party in New York, plush with celebrities and was "in really good spirits," said a friend. "Friendly, talkative and excited."

She attended an early screening of *Moulin Rouge* in New York as well, taking her time to stroll up a red carpet laid outside the Paris Theater. "I am fine now," she said to one reporter. "My kids are doing great. I have a lot of good support."

On another night she had a girls' night out, hanging at a hip bar with lesbian rocker Melissa Etheridge and, oddly enough, Meg Ryan, who split from her husband Dennis Quaid after a much-publicized affair with Kidman's old buddy Russell Crowe. People seemed to be pulling for Kidman — and against Cruise, who "for the first time ever ... appears to be getting some negative publicity," noted one writer.

And the work was still rolling in. Kidman went through with her commitment to *The Hours*, based on a Virginia Woolf novel. The distraction was no doubt welcomed by Nicole, who kicked her heels up at a London club at a cast party.

But while Kidman eased back into public life, it was full-steam ahead for Cruise.

He was deep into work on *Minority Report*, which brought him together for the first time with one of the few people in Hollywood who could match his own box-office clout: director Steven Spielberg, the man behind *Jaws, Close Encounters, Raiders of the Lost Ark* and *Schindler's List*.

Cruise and Spielberg came close to working together years before, when *Rain Man* was in development and Spielberg was set to direct. But Spielberg had to drop out to do another *Indiana Jones* picture. But the Cruise-Spielberg pairing was a studio dream — and it was inevitable they'd get together at some point.

Cruise approached Spielberg and director Scott Frank with the idea of *Minority Report* way back in 1997. The story — centered on a futuristic police unit which, using the ESP abilities of human but stunted "pre-cogs," stopped crimes before they happened — was based on a 1956 Philip K. Dick short story.

Cruise played John Anderton, top cop in the "pre-crime" unit, who becomes the target of the unit as part of a coverup by pre-crime's most impassioned supporter. When the pre-cogs "see"

Anderton committing a murder, the chase is on, and Anderton scurries for his freedom even as he tries to unravel the mystery of who he is going to kill — and why. Darkening the story is loss — Anderton's young son was abducted on his watch, leading to estrangement from his wife — and Anderton's own drug addiction.

Spielberg credited Cruise with helping to flesh out Anderton. Cruise, drawing on the emotions he felt for his own children, suggested that Anderton's motivation in stopping crime come at least partly from having lost a child himself.

"Tom came up with that to give the character complicated emotional baggage," Spielberg said.

"Anderton is a guy," Cruise said, "who is really running away from himself, a person who has a lot to hide in order to try to cope with his life. His emotional life is just kind of teetering — he lives for his work. And yet he has this whole undercurrent of what's happened to him in terms of the losses in his life and, ah ... ultimately he's faced with people trying to take everything away from him."

In the four years since Cruise first pitched *Minority Report* to Spielberg, they became fast friends. But that didn't mean the legendary director was any more privy to what was really going on in Cruise's life — or his mind — than the public at-large.

"I'm not someone who sits around talking about different problems, whatever happened to Nic and me. I just don't do that. That's just not who I am. But he's been a great friend to me," Cruise said of Spielberg.

"Tom never brought any of his personal misfortunes and/or achievements to the set," Spielberg concurred. "He kept everything that was happening in his life absolutely quiet. And when I was probing a little bit, Tom never said he wouldn't talk about it; Tom just found a way to deflect the conversations back to other things. He just dealt with it in his own way, and he dealt with it successfully. The most important thing to Tom was the emotional safety of his children. That was his main concern. That's what preoccupied him."

Colin Farrell, who played federal agent Witwer, said Cruise was nothing but focused, despite all that had to be on his mind during the filming of *Minority Report*.

"On the first day, swear to God, you look in his eyes and you f***in' know why he is where he is," Farrell said. "It's not luck, it's not pure ambition, it's not just hunger and drive and focus, though he has all those things — he's just a talented f***in' actor."

"The scenes I did with him, he just blew me away," said actress Samantha Morton, who played the main pre-cog in the film. "It shocked me because he was so amazing that I'd come out of character. No one's ever enticed me to do that, where I just want to watch what they're doing. I'd miss my cue sometimes."

Real life, meanwhile, continued to move ahead outside the studio. Though Nicole may not have been happy about it, Penelope spent weeks with Tom and the kids over the summer, first at Tom's rented home in Beverly Hills and later at the couple's home in Telluride, Colorado.

"She's been shocked by the way Tom has handled his romance with Penelope," a friend said. "I think Nicole hates the fact that Penelope has gotten along so well with the kids since Tom introduced them."

Reports claimed Tom and Penelope were getting ready to wed before the ink on Tom's divorce from Nicole was dry.

Tom and Nicole were officially divorced in early August, but issues remained to be ironed out. They said their goodbyes as a married couple Nov. 12, 2001. In a three-hour meeting in an attorney's office, the couple hashed out the final terms of their divorce and "interacted very well," according to Kidman's attorney.

The final score: According to reports, Nicole got the home in Pacific Palisades and the home in Sydney, while Tom got the place in Telluride plus his three airplanes, worth nearly $30 million. As for who got what from the rest of the $250 million fortune, the parties were tight-lipped. Nicole, though, was said to have received at least a $30 million settlement.

The couple also agreed to joint custody of the kids and agreed that all decisions on raising them will be made together. "Everyone was very pleased and happy," said Nicole's attorney, Sorrell Trope. Added a friend, "Nicole is relieved that everything is finally over and that she and Tom will have some kind of amicable relationship."

Cruise told a reporter, "We are great friends. She is someone who I love and always will."

But Cruise was weary of the public discussion about the divorce and was happy it was resolved without too much embarrassment to himself or the kids. "More than a few people were disappointed that ... we resolved these things," he said. "Things were sensationalized and things were drawn out and you just — it's life, man. Life is a fascinating ride and you just go, baby."

Nicole seemed to be getting with the Cruise program. "Divorce is divorce," she told a reporter. "Then you have to pick yourself up and move forward. And that's what I'm doing."

Though still in pain, Nicole was indeed attempting to move forward. She was linked with Counting Crows lead singer Adam Duritz, British pop star Robbie Williams, with whom she had a hit record in a quirky remake of the Frank Sinatra classic *Somethin' Stupid.*

But Nicole said she was just trying to have fun. "Anybody who's a single mother will understand that I don't have the time or energy to date right now," she said.

While Cruise and Crowe had to hustle to get an audience for *Vanilla Sky, The Others* got great reviews. When Nicole won a Golden Globe for *Moulin,* she used the opportunity to thank the people who, in her words, "stuck by me." That obviously didn't include her former husband.

"When Nicole mentioned all the people who 'stuck by her,' she was really sticking it to Tom," said a friend. "Nicole is a winner now — on her own — and she's not about to give Tom an ounce of credit for her success."

Typically, though, Cruise wasn't looking back. Perhaps what people told him about the great roles coming along in his 30s was correct. Or maybe the piling up of life experience was indeed adding depth to his acting.

"His performance is like a slow smolder," Spielberg said of Cruise's work in *Minority*

Report. "Every film Tom's made in the last couple years, from *Magnolia* to *Vanilla Sky* to the character he plays in *Minority Report* — I think these are all leaps. What I admire about Tom is that he really doesn't care much about the safety net."

Chapter 24

LIVE

CRUISE HAS COME a long way by staying in control of his career. Others call it discipline or focus, but the reality is that he is in control. He has always had a golden touch when it comes to choosing the films he's starred in, but there is no denying that he has achieved his ambition of growing as an actor, and as a person. There was always a certain palpable cold-bloodedness palpable in him — even as far back as

Rain Man — and that cool patina of ruthlessness has carried through the years and only become more evident in his work in *Magnolia* and *Minority Report*.

It's hard, of course, to separate Cruise from his roles, to imagine in hindsight how a movie would have played and what the box office might have been had someone else taken the role of Charlie Babbitt or Ron Kovic or John Anderton. But he has worked hard to shed the characterization that he was a lightweight, just a smile and in *Minority Report* he continued his upward mobility in the acting ranks.

"As Anderton," one reviewer wrote of Cruise's work in *Minority Report*, "Cruise shows how unfulfilled determination becomes the all-American burden. It may be one of his finest performances yet."

"It has been a long time since a Spielberg film felt so nimble, so unfettered, so free of self-cannibalizing," wrote another reviewer. "When he sheds his pandering mannerisms, he really is one of the most wittily dexterous filmmakers alive and he gets a fine, focused performance from Cruise."

Cruise Control also carries through in Tom's public image, which he so scrupulously tried to control over the years. But where the young Tom Cruise seemed to be begging someone — anyone

— to just love him and say nice things about him, as he hit 40, he seemed to get more defiant. He had an edge. His divorce from Kidman helped change his image from Nice Guy Tom to someone who was more cold and calculating and in it for himself — to someone who, like it or not, had more depth to his soul than he'd shown before.

"I do everything I can just to live my life," he said. "You do what you feel is right and what you know is correct in life and not worry about everything else."

Despite the rumors, the mysterious break with Nicole Kidman, the association with the controversial Church of Scientology, Cruise maintained a wide-eyed view of the industry he had conquered and, indeed, almost come to own.

"It's kind of amazing to me, you know, showing up on the set and working with Cameron Crowe and then showing up the next day working with Steven Spielberg," he said. "I am surprised. I'm surprised at how well things have gone.

"I still get excited," he said. "Days before I don't sleep and I only sleep a couple of hours before I start shooting."

He talked as though he'd been lucky — but of course there was much more to it than that. Unlike many actors and nonactors of his generation, there had been no crash and burn, no ugly rehab stints, no public meltdowns. Even during the one major public crisis of his life — his divorce from Nicole — he maintained discipline, kept things close to his vest, kept his image and his life under ... control.

Tom Cruise grew up before the world's eyes — but there seem to be few who really know him. Even Nicole, his wife for 10 years, seemed sucker-punched when he divorced her. He saved the essence of himself for himself and increasingly refused to allow his life to be become just another throwaway topic for pop culture. But even as he turned 40, even after the negative storm over his divorce from Nicole, even as his work took on a new form and depth, Cruise, the icon, remains.

"He has that deliciously, indescribable magic that cannot be analyzed or replicated," Spielberg summed up. "He is, in every sense, a movie star. The problem is he is such a big movie star that he has to work twice as hard to get you to forget that it's Tom Cruise up there onscreen. That's always been a handicap that he's worked under, but he's never shied away from the challenge of trying to make you forget who he is."

And Cruise the man? He was off to Japan, leaving behind a bubbling wake of gossip. Cruise was to play a 19th-century American who becomes involved in a Japanese civil war in *The Last Samurai* — and was no doubt pleased to step out of America's public eye for an extended length of time.

But the eyes of the world — and the United States — continued to be on him and on his relationship with Penelope Cruz. There were said to be ups and downs — reports that Penelope was not happy that Cruise bought a home in Sydney so he and Nicole could be together with the kids more often; that Penelope was jealous over a congratulatory phone call Cruise made to Kidman after she won the Oscar for best actress for *The Hours*; that Cruise dumped Penelope; that she had won him back. And — again — that they'd be married soon.

The world wanted to know when and if he'd marry Penelope — but it was unlikely it would get any help from Tom in figuring out where they stood. "We have no plans," he said, "despite what everyone says. I probably definitely will get married again at some point, because I enjoy that relationship." Even after the divorce from Nicole, he said, "I don't have regrets."

The last word, though, was that Tom was in no hurry to tie the knot — and indeed, might never marry again. "This divorce nearly killed him," a pal said.

Everyone in Hollywood continued to clamor for him to star in their pictures. He had been "mentioned to star" in half a dozen films, but the only certainty was that he'd be back as Ethan Hunt in a third *Mission: Impossible*.

All anyone really knew was that whatever happened, Cruise would be in control of his career and life, still living the lesson his mother taught him 25 years before on that frozen stretch of Canadian highway.

"I can't help thinking about where we all came from," he said. "I'll never forget traveling, leaving the country in the middle of the night in Canada, going to Kentucky. I never forget about that time ... but I have to say, also I'm looking forward to what's going to happen, because you just never know. For me, between 30 and 40 was a hell of a decade. Very busy and a lot of wonderful things happened to me. Even the tough things, you go, 'OK, you know, I'm here.'"

APPENDIX

FILMOGRAPHY

1. *Endless Love* (1981)
2. *Taps* (1981)
3. *The Outsiders* (1983)
4. *Losin' It* (1983)
5. *Risky Business* (1983)
6. *All the Right Moves* (1983)
7. *Legend* (1985)
8. *Top Gun* (1986)
9. *The Color of Money* (1986)
10. *Cocktail* (1988)
11. *Young Guns* (1988) (uncredited)
12. *Rain Man* (1988)
13. *Born on the Fourth of July* (1989)
14. *Days of Thunder* (1990)
15. *Far and Away* (1992)
16. *A Few Good Men* (1992)
17. *The Firm* (1993)
18. *Interview with the Vampire: The Vampire Chronicles* (1994)
19. *Mission: Impossible* (1996)
20. *Jerry Maguire* (1996)
21. *Eyes Wide Shut* (1999)
22. *Magnolia* (1999)
23. *Mission: Impossible II* (2000)
24. *Vanilla Sky* (2001)
25. *Minority Report* (2002)
26. *The Last Samurai* (2003) (post-production)
27. *Collateral* (2004) (pre-production)
28. *Mission: Impossible 3* (2005) (announced)